Enacting a Pedagogy of Kindness

Drawing from the lived experience of educators, this book explores the concept of a pedagogy of kindness through practical applications and strategies for teaching in higher education.

Conversational in tone, narrative-based and rich with practical stories, ideas and strategies, this book provides guidance to help educators shape their teaching. It covers all aspects of teaching in higher education, including curriculum design, delivery, marking and feedback. Each chapter describes a specific perspective on practical applications of kindness, including authentic strategies used to increase positivity and connection in teaching and learning. Through a series of case studies, it provides relatable examples that educators can apply to their practices as they navigate a dynamic and rewarding teaching environment.

This book will help educators who are keen to bring the joy back to their teaching and who want to connect with their students and see learning come alive again in higher education.

Airdre Grant is an experienced academic, author and educator with over 20 years' experience in teaching and learning. She worked in the Centre for Teaching and Learning at Southern Cross University for 15 years as an academic developer. In her role in the Learning Innovations team at Deakin University, Airdre supported academics' pedagogical practice in online teaching and learning environments through a focus on learning and assessment design. She is currently writing her third book, a novel about women in the workplace and the challenges they face maintaining their kindness and compassion.

Sharon Pittaway was an educator for over 20 years with experience teaching Preps to postgrads. As an English and Drama teacher, Sharon was keenly aware of the human-centred nature of the teaching–learning relationship. Her move into pre-service teacher education saw her continue to develop and refine her pedagogical practice and in her leadership roles, she supported others to examine and reflect on their own. Sharon's personal quest to be kind, initiated by the example of her grandmother, was at the forefront of her thinking and pedagogical practice throughout her years as an educator.

Enacting a Pedagogy of Kindness

A Guide for Practitioners in Higher Education

Edited by Airdre Grant and Sharon Pittaway

Routledge
Taylor & Francis Group

LONDON AND NEW YORK

First published 2025
by Routledge
4 Park Square, Milton Park, Abingdon, Oxon OX14 4RN

and by Routledge
605 Third Avenue, New York, NY 10158

Routledge is an imprint of the Taylor & Francis Group, an informa business

© 2025 selection and editorial matter, Airdre Grant and Sharon Pittaway; individual chapters, the contributors

The right of Airdre Grant and Sharon Pittaway to be identified as the authors of the editorial material, and of the authors for their individual chapters, has been asserted in accordance with sections 77 and 78 of the Copyright, Designs and Patents Act 1988.

British Library Cataloguing-in-Publication Data
A catalogue record for this book is available from the British Library

ISBN: 978-1-032-42915-1 (hbk)
ISBN: 978-1-032-42914-4 (pbk)
ISBN: 978-1-003-36488-7 (ebk)

DOI: 10.4324/9781003364887

Typeset in Galliard
by SPi Technologies India Pvt Ltd (Straive)

Airdre: This book is dedicated to all the students and colleagues who taught me how to be a better, kinder person and how to bring that into my professional practice. And to my family whose support and patience continue to teach me about the value of kindness and of love.

Sharon: I dedicate this book to all my former students who taught me what my acts of kindness felt like to them thus allowing me to develop and enact a more deliberate pedagogy of kindness.

Contents

Contributors

Debra Adelaide is an author, editor and critic who, until 2020, was an Associate Professor in the creative writing program at the University of Technology Sydney. She has published 18 books, including several novels and collections of short fiction and essays. Her most recent book is *Creative Writing Practice: Reflections on Form and Process* (co-edited with Sarah Attfield, Palgrave 2021).

Alan Borthwick OBE is an Emeritus Professor at the University of Southampton, UK, and an adjunct professor at both Southern Cross University and Queensland University of Technology in Australia. His academic research has focused on the sociology of the allied health professions. He was awarded an OBE in the 2016 Queen's Birthday Honours List, Honorary Life Membership of the Canadian Federation of Podiatric Medicine in 2012, a Meritorious Award (2008) and Citation (2014) of the Royal College of Podiatry and an Honorary Life Membership of the Prince Edward Island Podiatry Association in 2007.

Samantha Chang is an art historian by day, a classical musician by night and an educator always. She is a course instructor in the Department of Art History and the Faculty Liaison, Anti-Racist Pedagogies at the Centre for Teaching Support & Innovation, University of Toronto (U of T). Samantha currently serves as a co-chair of the Council of Ontario Educational Developers and the vice chair of the Teaching Assistant and Graduate Student Advancement in the Society for Teaching and Learning in Higher Education. In 2021, Samantha received the U of T Course Instructor Teaching Excellence Award and was shortlisted for the BIPOC (Black, Indigenous and People of Colour) Teaching Excellence Award in 2023.

Aris M. Clemons is an assistant professor of Spanish (Linguistics) in the department of World Languages and Cultures at the University of Tennessee, Knoxville. Her research is rooted in social change through an examination of how what appears to be common knowledge is often constructed and ideologically maintained. Importantly, she focuses on the linguistic mechanisms by which social categories are constructed and concretised in varying institutional contexts, including education and popular media. Her recent publications deal with Dominican race making in public forums, making space for bilingualism in English-only classrooms and expanding current disciplinary methods and theoretical frames towards liberatory justice for Black-language users.

Mark Cole is a recently retired principal teaching fellow at the University of Southampton, UK. His teaching interests include complex clinical conditions and healthcare in extreme environments. He previously worked in the NHS as a clinical manager. Mark has worked with professional, statutory and regulatory bodies providing strategic advice to shape national policy in relation to the delivery of allied health professional undergraduate and postgraduate training. He has a special interest in mentoring senior managers in academia and the NHS through periods of organisational change.

Edwin Creely is a senior lecturer in the Faculty of Education at Monash University. He is an experienced qualitative researcher with an interest in wellbeing and inclusion, creativity, literacy and language learning, digital pedagogies and technologies in education, artificial intelligence (AI), adult education and initial teacher education. His current projects include English language learning and digital literacies for adult migrants and refugees, creativity in initial teacher education, online and hybrid educational delivery in higher education, phenomenological research and lived experience and new models for thinking about generative AI in education. He is widely published in international journals and regularly presents at conferences.

Lachlan Forsyth is an Adjunct Associate Professor at Southern Cross University (SCU) in Australia. For over two decades, he has contributed to technological innovation, curriculum design and leadership in online education, community-based professional learning and academic development. Dr Forsyth's work is underpinned by a deep conviction to reflective practice, guided by self-inquiry, ecological systems thinking and the promotion of participatory collective learning. He is currently writing a folk musical for Anglo concertina, because that seemed like a good idea.

Kelly Galvin, a Senior Lecturer in the Learning Transformation Unit at Swinburne University, has a 27-year career spanning education and health industries. Kelly's doctoral research focused on developing an innovative approach to problem-based learning, designing an online decision-making tool to assist independent and group clinical reasoning development for undergraduate health science students. Kelly's ultimate goal in the field of higher education is to ensure that the learning experience is transformational, purpose-driven and guided by contextual and holistic indicators of quality, compliance and kindness.

Sandra Grace is a Professor in the Faculty of Health at Southern Cross University. She is Principal Fellow, Higher Education Academy, Chair of the Accreditation Committee and Deputy Chair of Academic Board (Teaching and Learning) at Southern Cross University. She has extensive experience as an educator, curriculum designer and promoter of the scholarship of teaching and learning. Sandra is also a health services researcher with research interests in models of care, interprofessional practice and education and integrative medicine. She is a member of the Chiropractic Australia Research Foundation and the Osteopathy Australia Research Committee and chairs the Academic Review Committee and Research Committee of the Australian Traditional Medicine Society.

Airdre Grant is an experienced academic, author and educator with over 20 years' experience in teaching and learning. She worked in the Centre for Teaching and Learning at Southern Cross University for 15 years as an academic developer. In her role in the Learning Innovations team at Deakin University, Airdre supported academics' pedagogical practice in online teaching and learning environments through a focus on learning and assessment design. She is currently writing her third book, a novel about women in the workplace and the challenges they face maintaining their kindness and compassion.

Matthew Harrison is an experienced teacher, researcher and digital creator with a passion for utilising technology to enhance social capacity building, belonging and inclusion in education. He has taught in Australia, South Korea and the United Kingdom at the primary, secondary and tertiary levels. Matthew is currently a member of the Learning Intervention team and the director of Professional and Continuing Education at the University of Melbourne Faculty of Education. He was awarded the Dyason Fellowship in 2020, the GEM Scott Teaching Fellowship and the International Society for Technology in Education 'Making IT Happen' award in 2023.

Jeff Janowick is a history professor at Lansing Community College, where he has taught for the last 24 years. He is an active participant in the college's student success and equity initiatives, and an advocate for the pedagogy of kindness. A dedicated teacher, he became more intentional in his practice of the pedagogy of kindness during the pandemic. He is committed to student success, faculty engagement and the community college mission.

Abbey MacDonald is a Senior Lecturer in Arts Education and Graduate Research Co-ordinator in the School of Education at the University of Tasmania. Her interdisciplinary arts-based research is used to inform arts, cultural and education policy development and museum and gallery education resources. She partners with environmental conservation and social change organisations to tackle some of the most pressing challenges educators face today. Abbey is the president of Australia's peak body for visual art education, Art Education Australia and a member of Australia's National Advocates for Arts Education council.

Jacqueline Mackaway is a social researcher interested in the sociology of education and work, with a particular interest in equity, diversity and inclusion in both education and workplace settings. Jacqueline teaches at the School of Social Science at Macquarie University, Australia. She has a passion for experiential-based learning and has published extensively on work-integrated learning. In recognition of her contribution to teaching, she received Macquarie University's PACE Staff Award 2022. In a prior professional life, she worked in human resource management across a range of sectors and had responsibilities in Australia and internationally.

Rachel Matthews is Head of School for Design at Australian College of the Arts in Melbourne. She is a researcher and educator who sees design as a force for good, advocating for responsible design curriculum supported by a critical yet hopeful learning context. Rachel's research concerns the networked conditions of contemporary communications and its power to influence consumer tastes and behaviours. Her current interests examine new notions of fashion marketing as alternative communication practices capable of hastening a green transition in the fashion industry.

Tim Moss is Dean of the Australian College of the Arts and finds that although he's worked in higher education for almost 25 years, much of his work doesn't fit neatly into the 'traditional' academic boxes of research interests, teaching expertise, and service. He hopes that his writing here will make clear his context (Australian higher education in an independent, arts-focused provider), his experiences (predominantly teacher education and arts education), and his ongoing professional interests (improving higher education and arts education through collective and culture-led approaches to leadership). Tim has his own arts practice as a photographer and has recently begun to try his hand at drawing.

Jo Munn is an academic in the Centre for Teaching and Learning at Southern Cross University. Specialising in academic development, she is passionate about access to, and success of, non-traditional students in tertiary education in regional areas. Jo believes in the transformative power of education for individuals and communities alike and with this recognises the responsibility of educators to provide authentic learning experiences that adapt to the status quo.

Charlotte Overgaard is a tertiary educator committed to pedagogies of kindness (PoK), with a developing publishing record on PoK and always trialling and documenting new initiatives to enact PoK. Charlotte currently teaches at the Department of Politics and Society at Aalborg University, Denmark. Her other research interests besides PoK are many and varied. One strand of research is organised around questions about how volunteer care work is organised and valued in society overall and within organisations. Another strand focuses on migrant workers, including the experiences of migrant care workers, the housing conditions of international students and the work environment of migrants in the construction sector.

Ameena L. Payne is a strategic scholarship holder at Deakin University's Centre for Research in Assessment and Digital Learning. Her doctoral research aims to better understand the lived feedback experiences of culturally, ethnically and linguistically diverse postgraduate coursework students in Australia. Ameena is a recipient of the Alison Lee 'Theory in Educational Research' Scholarship (2023) as well as her alma mater's Outstanding Young Alumna Award (2022). Her recent publications include 'Humanising Feedback Encounters: A Qualitative Study of Relational Literacies for Teachers Engaging in Technology-Enhanced Feedback' (with Rola Ajjawi and Jessica Holloway) in Assessment and Evaluation in Higher Education.

Sharon Pittaway was an educator for over 20 years with experience teaching Preps to postgrads. As an English and Drama teacher, Sharon was keenly aware of the human-centred nature of the teaching-learning relationship. Her move into pre-service teacher education saw her continue to develop and refine her pedagogical practice and in her leadership roles, she supported others to examine and reflect on their own. Sharon's personal quest to be kind, initiated by the example of her grandmother, was at the forefront of her thinking and pedagogical practice throughout her years as an educator.

Lauren E. Stephens is a Lecturer and the EDGE Coordinator in the Department of Parks, Recreation and Tourism Management at Clemson University. She is passionate about student learning and engagement, where her approach to teaching is grounded in viewing her students as people first and students second. Through enacting tenants of the pedagogy of kindness, Stephens strives to form meaningful relationships with her students through the creation of safe spaces where tough questions are welcomed, mutual respect is established, and trust is earned. Her research explores the intersection of relationships, social media and body image in the sport context.

Mieke Witsel is a social scientist with expertise in positive psychology, higher education and transcultural teaching. She has enjoyed university teaching for more than three decades, earning recognition through national and international awards for teaching, community engagement and meeting students' needs. Dr. Witsel is presently the Director of the Centre for Teaching and Learning at Southern Cross University. Her pragmatic and scholarly approach uses transformative, strengths-based methods to empower educators, boost academic capacity and champion the approaches that foster student success. Because really, in the end, it is the students who matter most.

Chapter 1

An introduction to a Pedagogy of Kindness

Airdre Grant and Sharon Pittaway

Kindness is central to inspirational and transformative educational practice.

Many educators have given thought to the necessity of kindness in teaching and what it means to be kind in practical and effective ways. They have written and talked about how to sustain their commitment to their students and their discipline, knowing the many pressures and practicalities which impact their practice. In 1928, Eugene Bertram Willard noted that "kindness is a greater factor in pedagogy than some teachers seem ready to admit ... kindness, in and out of the classroom, has an untold power of developing not only its like, but actual good in others" (p. 157). We believe that kindness lies at the heart of all good practice in any endeavour. It gets tested and challenged, and yet, without it, teaching runs the risk of becoming mechanical and dehumanised. Simply put, kindness matters.

A pedagogy of kindness is akin to what other scholars call love. bell hooks (2004) wrote that when teachers "teach with love, combining care, commitment, knowledge, responsibility, respect, and trust, we are often able to enter the classroom and go straight to the heart of the matter, which is knowing what to do on any given day to create the best climate for learning" (p. 134). Teaching that has a pedagogical and philosophical basis in love means it 'inherently and unconditionally honours who [students] are' (Clingan, 2015, p. 5).

Cate Denial's article, published in 2019, drew attention to the term 'pedagogy of kindness' (PoK), which she defined as 'believing students and believing in them'. Denial's article drew us back to earlier work by Sue Clegg and Stephen Rowland titled *Kindness in Pedagogical Practice and Academic Life* in which they stated that kindness is "both commonplace yet unremarked and that ... it is subversive of neo-liberal values" (2010, p. 719). Their conclusion was that kindness cannot be regulated or prescribed.

But it can be enacted.

For this book, we invited contributors to share their experiences of enacting a pedagogy of kindness into their practice in higher education. We wanted to hear the voices of our colleagues who are working to make a difference to their students' learning and lives through their pedagogy, and to the lives of their

DOI: 10.4324/9781003364887-1

colleagues. The narratives in this book illustrate the various ways they have enacted kindness as a pedagogical practice, whether dealing with students, colleagues, the institutions of which they're a part, or themselves.

We also thought it important to share something of our own stories to offer insights into our personal journey toward cultivating kindness as a pedagogical practice.

Airdre

I worked for many years as an academic developer in a university teaching and learning centre. My work focused on the uplift of teaching practice. When working with engineers, midwives and other professionals, I discovered that many were employed to teach without teaching qualifications; they were employed as subject matter experts. The thinking was that, as long as someone was an expert in a particular field, they could teach. It was no surprise, therefore, that their teaching focused on delivering content (what they knew) rather than on students. Many floundered and tended to teach as they were taught. This was exacerbated when they were asked to teach in non-lecture-based formats, teach units written by somebody else or use unfamiliar platforms such as Blackboard or Canvas. It was while working with me that they began to understand the complexity and challenges of pedagogy. This caused me to reflect on the importance of kindness and what it meant in terms of pedagogical practice. I could see that a shift in mindset was needed. Teaching is more than the delivery of content and being kind; it encompasses being attuned to students, understanding students' paths, contexts and the skills and knowledge they bring to the discipline. This work had its challenges; these new academics would often be resistant to shift from thinking about content to thinking about students and unsure about how to develop a positive relationship with students. It caused me to think about how I enacted kindness in my own practice.

In my doctoral work, my supervisor taught me the difference between praise and encouragement. He rarely praised me yet consistently encouraged me. It was an object lesson in how to guide a person to do a difficult task and provide feedback in such a way that the learner could gain the skills needed for the task. The skilful guidance and giving of feedback were instructive. My supervisor demonstrated how to enact kindness throughout the long doctoral journey through patience and good listening. Praise would not have served me, but my supervisor's consistent encouragement taught me about the unique blend of kindness and authority, which is central to healthy respect and striving towards work of a high standard. His encouragement was valuable to me, even when he was correcting me or steering me back on course when I had veered off into an area which was interesting but not relevant. For example, he showed me how a whole chapter, of which I was quite proud, was not relevant and had to go. His approach to telling me was firm yet kind. I trusted his guidance.

Later, I supervised a challenging doctoral candidate who resisted any suggested change to their writing. They eventually changed supervisors, and as hurtful as that was at the time, it prompted a conversation with a colleague about kindness and self-care. I came to understand that not all situations can be resolved happily and to everybody's satisfaction. What might look and feel like kindness to one person may not be experienced in the same way by others.

At a private college, I taught a student who was struggling. I felt very sorry for this student and at one stage awarded their assessment work a pass when really it should have failed. My misguided kindness did the student no service. She enrolled in the next subject, failed and left the institution. I realised that what I viewed as kindness wasn't, and it also wasn't helpful. If anything, I failed her, by being 'nice' and coddling her rather than supporting her to develop her strengths. I had a lot to learn about the muscular realities of kindness.

Sharon

I experienced many unkind teachers throughout my years at school but not too many who were kind. Metaphors of warfare (the teacher as soldiers off to battle the enemy/students) were more prevalent than metaphors aligned with kindness. In my late 20s, I enrolled in a teaching degree, and during a particularly tough final-year placement, I reflected at length on pedagogical kindness as I came to understand myself as a teacher. The students were from homes characterised by intergenerational under/unemployment, crime, drug use, domestic violence and low educational achievement. What did it mean to enact kindness in this context? Was it kind to encourage students to participate in the local drama festival, or was it kind to allow them to withdraw when they felt anxious about performing? Was it kind to establish boundaries for class interactions designed to work towards creating a space in which all students felt safe to express themselves – or was that me imposing my will? I certainly wasn't kind to one Grade 7 student who sat waiting patiently while I struggled to stop the boys from spitting at each other and hiding under rostra blocks. Was I kind? It was a question I wrestled with throughout the placement and on into my high school teaching career. When I started teaching pre-service teachers at university, I again had cause to reflect on my practice. I tended to ask a lot of questions and many students felt this was an unkindness. 'Just tell us what to do', they'd cry when I'd answer their questions with more questions. To paraphrase Stephen Brookfield, the sincerity of our intentions does not guarantee the kindness of our practice.

******

So, what exactly do we mean by kindness, and specifically, a PoK? As we understand it, a PoK is fundamentally a philosophical approach: an intellectual and emotional position that embraces compassionate pedagogy and self-care and incorporates a deeply held commitment to students in teaching and learning interactions that transcends kind intentions.

When we introduced this concept to our colleagues in a Faculty of Business a few years ago, some initially misconstrued it as a call to 'go soft' on students, using terms like 'spoon-feeding' and 'handholding' – expressions that carry negative connotations in higher education – and thought it entailed lowering academic standards, leniency and allowing students to get away with anything. Some of our colleagues held the belief that students should be metaphorically thrown into the deep end and left to sink or swim, arguing that this mirrors the challenges of the real world and should thus be replicated in the learning environment.

A PoK is not the same as 'being nice' or 'being lenient' to students, and it does not mean we lower academic standards or expectations. It's a philosophical approach which informs all aspects of teaching practice, including supervision, curriculum design, giving and receiving feedback and much more. A pedagogy of kindness revolves around creating a supportive and inclusive learning environment where educators consider students' well-being and personal growth alongside academic achievement. According to Denial (2019), it's, first of all, a way of thinking about students. If we treat students with suspicion and distrust and view them through a deficit lens, it can be very easy to take a combative approach to teaching. Fiona Rawle (2021) argues that if learning and wellness are our goals, then "we need to build from a foundation of kindness".

Brene Brown, known for her work on vulnerability and leadership, notes that 'clear is kind', and our contention is that clarity is another important component of a PoK. Clarity is vital when developing the structure of a course as well as the structure of individual units/subjects within that course. In Chapter 2, Mieke Witsel and Lachlan Forsyth note that when there is clarity (of purpose, values and an understanding of students' needs) educators can more clearly align their decision-making and planning with students' most fundamental requirements.

Curriculum design, as Mieke and Lachlan discuss, sets up conditions for kindness in other areas of the educational endeavour. In Chapter 3, Jo Munn and Rachel Matthews share (very different) stories about enacting kindness in assessment design. Jo's focus is on generative artificial intelligence, a contentious, fast-moving area impacting education, learning and assessment in potentially unknowable ways. She asks what it means to enact a PoK in a context in which distrust and suspicion are rife. Rachel's case study is quite different. In it she shares an example of an assessment task which invites students to investigate 'big existential issues' in fashion and sustainability through an examination of their personal relationship with fashion. These stories provide insights into the sorts of questions educators grapple with and the ways they foreground kindness in their thinking and the solutions to some of the issues they encounter when designing assessment tasks.

Due to the various demands on an academic's time, their focus may be directed towards considering what they want students to learn rather than devising activities and tasks that allow students to develop and then demonstrate knowledge acquisition, skill development and enhanced understanding/conceptual clarity. In this way, a PoK aligns with a student- or learner-centred approach to teaching. In this approach, the learner is the focus rather than the academic or the content. In Chapter 4, learning designer Kelly Galvin illustrates how kindness applies just as much to working with colleagues as to working with students. She describes working with an academic who had not considered other ways of teaching beyond a weekly 'content dump'; his focus was on what he needed to do rather than on how students were learning and how they might demonstrate their learning. Kelly notes that her work, which was primarily for an online course, helped her develop an understanding that learning design is enriched when it has a foundation in kindness.

Chapter 5 contains case studies of educators who enact a pedagogy of kindness in their teaching. These educators illustrate ways they strike a balance between creating a nurturing environment that expresses care, compassion, and empathy for their students and one that seeks to challenge students intellectually, professionally and academically. The case studies demonstrate various ways of empowering students to become not only knowledgeable and skilful but also compassionate and responsible individuals, preparing them for success in both academic and real-world pursuits.

Teaching and learning in physical spaces is one thing, but online learning and teaching is quite another. It can feel isolating for students and lead to a sense of detachment from peers and the teacher. In Chapter 6, Abbey MacDonald highlights some of the challenges of enacting a PoK in the online environment and raises important distinctions between kindness that is 'intended, enacted and felt'. Abbey asks whether our kindness is felt in the ways we intend and enact it and whether we can be comfortable not knowing the answer to that question.

We have already noted that a PoK is not about 'going soft' on students or 'giving' them what they want. It is not necessarily about keeping students 'satisfied' – that inadequate measure of teacher success used by many institutions. There are, as Airdre has mentioned, muscular realities to kindness as a pedagogical practice, one of which is reframing failure. Ed Creely picks up this notion in Chapter 7, where he contends that "failure … is a vital component of a PoK". He argues that failure allows students to "become agential and affords them an opportunity to be self-directed", important skills for any learner.

In Chapter 8, Ameena Payne and Aris Clemons provoke us to think about the importance of recognising our own political beliefs, values and goals as they apply to enacting a PoK. They share stories of the problem of viewing students through a deficit lens (an idea introduced in Chapter 5) and argue that those educators who have not examined their own values and assumptions ('uncritical educators') often understand their role as primarily about helping students overcome the perceived deficits of their background, class, race and socio-economic status. Ameena and Aris exhort educators to critically examine the assumptions and values that underpin their teaching as a means of reaching clarity about why they teach in the way they do and to understand where and how a PoK might better serve them and their students.

Our capacity for kindness can be extinguished by the neo-liberal values underpinning institutional structures, policies, and processes. The pressures of a changeable world and administrative overload can serve to frustrate academics and obliterate their delight in teaching and connection with students. In Chapter 9, Tim Moss shares his experience of explicitly developing a kind institutional culture, one that emphasises 'heart, authenticity and insight' as fundamental principles of teaching, learning and working together.

Not all institutions possess the capability, the inclination, or perhaps the freedom, to explicitly foster the kind of culture Tim describes in Chapter 9. The educational landscape is laden with pressures that detract from the innate joy of teaching. Timelines, deadlines, institutional constraints and short-term contracts cast a shadow over educators, compelling them to prioritise administrative tasks and quantitative outcomes over the quality of their teaching and interactions with students. These burdens can lead to burnout, a sense of detachment and a loss of enthusiasm for the profession: kindness can be easily extinguished. We therefore conclude the book by sharing stories of how academics have enacted self-care.

We acknowledge that prioritising self-compassion and maintaining personal well-being should not be solely an individual's responsibility, however, as Alan Borthwick OBE and Mark Cole note in Chapter 10, "organisations need the empathy and understanding of individuals to interpret the rules with thoughtfulness and care. Surviving the harsh world of academia so often depends on the benevolence and foresight of good leaders and effective managers". The stories in this chapter illustrate the benefits of self-care, not only for the individuals themselves but also for their students. Through enacting self-care, these academics were able to implement and sustain a PoK.

The choice to infuse our teaching with empathy, compassion, and respect is not just a theoretical one; it has real and profound consequences for our students and the world they shape. A PoK can help pave the way for a more inclusive, just and compassionate educational landscape that has the power to transform lives. We contend that this is critical in pedagogy as changes to the nature of academic work continue to challenge personal and professional principles. We, and our contributors, are deeply committed and passionate about education and pedagogy. As you read the stories of enacting a pedagogy of kindness, we encourage you to consider this 'subversive' act and ask, why not be kind?

What might be lost if we enact kindness as a pedagogical practice?

What might be gained?

References

Clegg, S., & Rowland, S. (2010). Kindness in pedagogical practice and academic life. *British Journal of Sociology of Education*, *31*(6), 719–735. https://doi.org/10.1080/01425692.2010.515102

Clingan, J. (2015). A pedagogy of love. *Journal of Sustainability Education*, *9*. https://www.susted.com/wordpress/content/a-pedagogy-of-love_2015_03/

Denial, C. (2019). A pedagogy of kindness. *Hybrid Pedagogy*. https://hybridpedagogy.org/pedagogy-of-kindness/

hooks, b. (2004). *Teaching community: A pedagogy of hope*. Routledge.

Rawle, F. (2021). A pedagogy of kindness: The cornerstone for student learning and wellness. *Times Higher Education*. https://www.timeshighereducation.com/campus/pedagogy-kindness-cornerstone-student-learning-and-wellness

Willard, E. B. (1928). What constitutes a true teacher? *Journal of Education*, *107*(10), 301–301. https://doi.org/10.1177/002205742810701010

Chapter 2

Kindness in course and curriculum design

Mieke Witsel and Lachlan Forsyth

There are many professional contexts through which to explore, experience and progress a pedagogy of kindness in higher education. For both of us, the most recent comes in the form of academic and managerial leadership in a Centre for Teaching and Learning: Lachlan as a former director and Mieke as the current director. Fulfilling such a position certainly challenges assumptions and perceptions of what it means to enact kindness within the complex ecology of learning and teaching in higher education. Most fundamentally, in the daily obligation to deliberate and negotiate on what really matters and what doesn't, what should be supported and what must be constrained, the director role has held a mirror to our souls with a recurring challenge that could be summarised 'While this may be effective for learning and teaching, is it kind?' It seems fitting, therefore, to begin with two confessional statements of a sort.

Mieke

I think I'm a kind person. But is acting in a kind manner enough to enact a pedagogy of kindness? After 35 years as a university 'lecturer', I still love my work: the process of enhancing student learning and of positively influencing student lives. I've taught in Europe, the UK, Asia and Australia, focusing on teaching and learning, positive psychology/sociology and communication. My PhD looked at the experiences of academics teaching in transcultural contexts. I taught for several decades and received an Australian Award for University Teaching Citation. Mostly, now, I lead the academic team responsible for enhancing professional learning at Southern Cross University's Centre for Teaching and Learning. Within this role, I help shape curriculum policy and processes.

A pedagogy of kindness underpins my curriculum decisions, although these choices may not always align with the preferences of fellow academics. I distinctly remember the strong reactions from my colleagues when I proposed online assignment submission and marking several years ago – an option that substantially benefitted students by reducing costs and saving travel time.

DOI: 10.4324/9781003364887-2

However, my peers rebelled; they saw me as a "meanie" for introducing online grading, tying them to computer screens instead of allowing them to use pen and paper comfortably on their sofas.

Lachlan

For over two decades, I've been committed to supporting learning and teaching across a wide range of contexts. Beginning with an arts-based educational business, I was led by my passion for collective and peer-based learning to a PhD that explored this phenomenon in blended and online communities for teacher professional development. This established my ecological sensibilities for educational systems, cognition and learning: a frame of reference that has underpinned my work as an eLearning designer, lecturer, curriculum designer and then director of the Centre for Teaching and Learning. Yet my focus on principled, values-based approaches to learning and teaching, including a political ecological basis for ethical decision-making, has not rescued me from the dilemma of determining what compassion and kindness really mean in these complex educational ecologies. So, I'll just get straight to the point....

I've been accused of being unkind. I was informed in no uncertain terms that in seeking to establish more effective systems and processes that aligned to our team's and institution's core values and strategic directions, I had lost sight of the human dimension. This was despite my continual focus on the need to support student and staff wellbeing and my intent to ensure we operated from integrity and our shared values, purpose and community. The accusation was confronting for me because it again foregrounded my own self-inquiry regarding kindness. Yet, it was also a reminder, coming as it did with its own bag of values and perspectives, that accusations of being unkind can be 'loaded' as much as any other label. Ultimately, it deepened my interest in understanding what an authentic pedagogy of kindness looks like within the complex ecology of higher education, across multiple scales and nested systems. This has been an inquiry underpinned by a desire to deepen my own practice of kindness. It has also been a countermeasure against using a pedagogy of kindness as a pedestal from which to label others as unkind. Perhaps the burden of leadership through the uncertainties, traumas and change fatigue brought on by the COVID-19 pandemic, catastrophic community floods and significant institutional change has affirmed the sense that we are all in this together, working to establish what true compassion and kindness look like in practice. Confessional over.

Kindness is frequently associated with human behaviour. It is applied at an individual level and not generally perceived as applicable to a broader institution. Perhaps this is unsurprising, given the apparent gulf between the practices and behaviours regularly attributed to kindness and the swathe of bureaucratic processes underpinning institutional governance. These can range from mandatory rules, policies and procedures to optional guidelines and other processes, fuelled by a need to regulate, support and enable people and systems. In the case of tertiary education institutions, these systemic processes can positively or adversely affect the student experience, often in ways that are deeply impactful on a student's life, sense of efficacy and wellbeing. It seems appropriate therefore to apply our notions and measures of kindness across all levels of an educational institution. It is our experience and contention that when an institution embeds a pedagogy of kindness into its approaches to policy development, student experience and, thus, student outcomes can benefit. We focus here on how such an approach can inform a pedagogy of kindness associated with course design in higher education.

A pedagogy of kindness is a teaching philosophy that emphasises compassion, care, empathy, and respect to foster better learning and a supportive environment. Such kindnesses can be applied to various aspects of pedagogy. Pedagogy in higher education encompasses multiple curriculum elements, from assessment strategies and technology integration to the physical, cognitive and emotional learning environment. While pedagogy is often discussed in terms of those synchronous exchanges between teacher and student during class, it is crucial to recognise that course design plays a significant role in shaping the teacher's ability to enact a pedagogy of kindness.

Course design predominantly precedes the teaching process, enabling and constraining the approaches taken by the teacher. As curriculum and course designers, we are responsible for proposing what matters 'downstream', to the student, the teacher, the discipline, the community and the institution, among others. It is a process of 'relevance realisation' (after Vervaeke et al., 2012) that, when aligned to a pedagogy of kindness, can foreground and enable meaningful relationships that recognise the depth and fullness of our students. For us, course design is, therefore, a vitally important component in enacting a pedagogy of kindness: one that, in the words of Malti (2021), "is a considerate stance towards life, which creates meaning and purpose. It involves a deep concern (i.e., compassion) for both others and the self and, as such, reflects an appreciation of the dignity of every human being" (p. 3). However, course design can seem to do the exact opposite.

As teachers, we have probably all experienced the sense that we are constrained in our ability to support deep learning and development due to pre-established system conditions, often related to curriculum and course design. We sense moments where our pedagogy could be deepened and more adequately supported through kind action, yet the opportunity to follow those moments can be lost due to pre-established system constraints and assumptions. While we recognise that enacting kindness across an educational system must involve vigilance and awareness of hierarchical power relations and influences (Clegg & Rowland, 2010), when it comes to the distributed nature of course design, we have found it unhelpful to fall back into the well-trodden tropes of 'us' (e.g., teachers) versus 'them' (e.g., curriculum designers), 'top down' (e.g., accreditation committees) versus 'bottom up' (e.g., other staff), 'in class' (e.g., teacher's role including enacted curriculum) versus 'out of class' (e.g., pre-established curriculum and system factors). Instead, we seek to conceive of this challenge as one that is shared across nested levels and the integrated phases of curriculum design, teaching and learning, regardless of what position we fulfil in the educational system.

Certainly, we recognise that course design can often be compliance-driven, potentially hindering the depth of academic, social and emotional considerations underpinning the resulting design. We have seen the result of course design that becomes a practice of 'going through the motions' or 'box ticking' and have probably witnessed first-hand how such 'hoop jumping' rarely leads to educational designs that truly enact the principles espoused, often failing to support or scaffold students adequately, without the Herculean effort of a committed teacher going above and beyond the call of duty.

Sometimes, and understandably so, academics and teachers view course design policies and procedures with a jaded, bureaucracy-fatigued lens (generally, this sort of stuff bores people to death). It need not be so. One way to enable a pedagogy of kindness through course design is to establish and then genuinely support learning and teaching policies and procedures that reflect kindness within the institution's values and principles. In our institutional experience, a key element in this process that helps overcome the 'top down' versus 'bottom up' binary is to ensure each faculty is involved in the establishment of these principles while also being supported (over years) to interpret and enact them within their disciplines.

Based on our experience, this supported academic and curriculum design process helps us become more attuned and responsive as educational and disciplinary experts to each student's unique challenges. We contend that when both institutional support and academic support are integrated into the design process right from the initial stages of course development and throughout each phase, it naturally leads us to align our decision-making and planning with the most fundamental requirements of our students and establishes the right conditions for a natural consideration of kindness in education.

By considering the larger educational context and the student experience beyond just the moments in the classroom, we can establish a more comprehensive approach to pedagogy that fosters a culture of kindness in higher education. That way, kindness becomes embedded and not the sole responsibility of the individual academic teacher. Again, this requires an academic model that recognises students' lived experiences and implements inherently compassionate learning and teaching policies and procedures as a foundation for course design and other educational design and governance elements.

This chapter focuses on the vital role course design elements play in illustrating and enabling a pedagogy of kindness beyond the synchronous expression of kindness within classroom interaction, thereby empowering students in their educational journey.

The Southern Cross Model

Between 2019 and 2023, our institution, Southern Cross University (SCU), established a suite of new policies, articulating the institution's values and principles to be interpreted and enacted by each faculty and discipline. In the following, we explore how this innovative curriculum approach, the Southern Cross Model, illustrates and enables a pedagogy of kindness.

The Southern Cross Model contains key ingredients that embody a pedagogy of kindness in course design. These include a course design process that is constructively aligned, replacing lectures, promoting active learning and eliminating exams as a form of assessment. Additionally, the number of assessments for each unit is limited to three or fewer and academic assessment calibration is to be conducted before submission. Students are presented with timely, online unit outlines and learning site readiness.

The model uses a focused six-week term with a maximum enrolment of two units per term to help students deepen their disciplinary studies and make the most of their time. Together, these elements of curriculum design inherently promote and facilitate a pedagogy of kindness. We explore each of these ingredients in the following paragraphs.

Constructively align the curriculum

From SCU Course Design Policy, Design Principle 3: Accredited courses and units must be designed using constructive alignment of expected learning outcomes with content, learning activities and assessment.

Constructive alignment, initiated by Biggs in 1999, offers students clear and specific learning outcomes, providing them with a sense of direction and purpose. A constructively aligned course integrates and scaffolds the key course learning outcomes and transferable skills so valuable in professional contexts. Once the intended learning outcomes are defined for each subject, the academic selects learning and teaching activities that support students in achieving these outcomes. Assessments are designed to directly address the learning outcomes, ensuring alignment, and using appropriate rubrics. Everyone involved knows where they're headed and what they need to show along the way. Clarity ensues.

Research by Rust et al. (2005) demonstrates that courses designed using constructive alignment led to lower attrition rates, higher student satisfaction and better learning outcomes than courses that do not follow this approach. In their meta-analysis, Biggs and Tang (2011) highlight the positive student outcomes associated with constructive alignment. Therefore, starting with a constructively aligned curriculum can create a supportive and positive learning environment that fosters student growth and development at the university.

Constructive alignment of the curriculum is crucial for the best interests of students and aligns with the key elements of a pedagogy of kindness. At SCU, the curriculum policy highlights the significance of constructive alignment as a key principle in curriculum design. This approach ensures that the proposed learning activities and assessment tasks directly align with the learning outcomes established at the unit and course levels. In its clarity and direction, this approach embodies a pedagogy of kindness by prioritising students' time and focusing on knowledge and skills relevant to their degree.

Does it always achieve this in practice? Not always. At our institution, the bedding down of constructive alignment as a deep, systemic foundation of our academic model has been a cultural shift and one that continues to require academic support, professional development, and continuous improvement. It seems worth recognising, albeit tangentially, that SCU's Accreditation Committee, the academic governance body most directly overseeing this change process, has modelled a high standard of kindness and compassion throughout the bedding down of constructive alignment across the institution. Perhaps such modelling, with its deep consideration of the needs of faculty, course design teams, academics and students, has also contributed to enacting a pedagogy of kindness throughout the course design process. Again, such considerations may help shift us away from the 'us' versus 'them' and 'top down' versus 'bottom up' binaries that can undermine compassion by keeping us focused on the 'other' that is stopping 'us' from being kind and appropriate to our students.

We have also experienced a range of misunderstandings regarding constructive alignment, which leads course designers to consider the practice restrictive on teachers and students: a claim that would seem to run counter to our notion that the curriculum approach supports a deep kindness and respect for all parties. It is helpful to review these misunderstandings regarding the various stages of the design process:

- Unit Design and Curriculum Mapping. When course designers are unfamiliar with constructive alignment, it is common for extraneous content to be prioritised in the planning phase rather than a well-aligned instructional design attuned to the core needs of the discipline and student. This leads to the cramming of content and a lack of appropriate scaffolding for students. It can also result in a forced mashing of assessment at the end of the unit, to cover all the content chosen rather than aligning the assessment to the learning outcomes. The result is student feedback stating that there is too much content in the unit and students experiencing assessments as unnecessarily complex or irrelevant to the learning outcomes.
- Writing Learning Outcomes. Constructive alignment does not constrain the establishment of learning outcomes but, rather, supports a strong integration between these learning goals and the students' learning experiences, including their assessments. Yet misunderstandings can arise here, with academics confusing the need for clear, measurable learning outcomes with a perceived requirement to make these learning outcomes too restrictive for

the needs of teachers and students. Specific, measurable learning outcomes can still be pitched to allow flexibility and autonomy for teachers and students while also targeting the core learning requirements of the discipline or subject.

- Assessment and Rubric Design. In our experience, rubrics are often delegated to the end of the assessment design phase and accorded little importance. For students, this can result in the sense of an 'unexpected item in the bagging area'. SCU has established a policy that mandates assessment rubrics, with an associated assessment moderation guideline that supports marking teams to understand and utilise the rubric effectively during the assessment process.

Banish lectures and apply active learning

Under SCU Assessment, Teaching and Learning Policy, Teaching and Learning Principle 3 (Learning is supported by a consistent teaching delivery approach across the University):

> (16) Our teaching is complemented by class learning, which consists of carefully planned, scheduled, interactive learning experiences that move beyond first exposure to new knowledge and skills and place greater emphasis on active-learning such as application, problem-solving, critiquing, simulating, group inquiry and creating.

We've probably all experienced the thrill of a dynamic and charismatic lecturer, and there are certainly online examples of captivating teachers who excel at the pedagogy of the lecture hall. Yet, as a student, how much did you remember from the lectures you sat through? You probably remembered the academic at the podium, as a person, especially if they were engaging and entertaining and had relatable stories to convey. But how much did you remember of the subject content? Did you experience interminably boring lectures? To what extent did those lectures consolidate your learning?

Active learning as a course design strategy is eminently kinder to students than traditional models. Research shows that the information transmission strategies inherent in a lecture-based model are not conducive to student success: "failure rates under traditional lecturing increase by 55% over the rates observed under active learning" (Freeman et al., 2014). Active learning can involve discussions, problem-solving tasks, service learning, debates, group work, simulations, role-playing and problem-based learning scenarios. These typically engage the participants in a sense of 'flow' characterised by deep meaning, insight and creativity (Csikszentmihalyi, 1990). Not only are such learning experiences more absorbing and engaging than passive learning, but they also recognise students as full, embodied human beings: respectful of their own awareness, insight and emotional needs. This approach reflects the pedagogy of kindness while also aligning well with contemporary cognitive science regarding the cultivation of insight, wisdom and empathetic understanding through deeply embodied and fully engaged processes of learning and development (e.g., Vervaeke & Ferraro, 2013). More bluntly, education without meaning and deep engagement is boring. Boredom is anathema to learning and is inherently unkind to students. Active learning activities promote student engagement and deep learning.

Eliminate exams and apply compassionate, authentic assessment

Under SCU Assessment, Teaching and Learning Procedures (Section 3 – 'Assessment Design and Validation')

> (14) Assessment is designed to be authentic for students wherever possible; for example, setting tasks that are performance-based, practice-based; industry-relevant; work-integrated; project-based; self-reflective or dilemma-based.

> (25) In the Southern Cross Model, authentic assessment tasks are preferred over examinations, as per clause (14).

> (26) Examinations must only be set as an assessment task where there are documented and justifiable external accreditation reasons approved by the relevant Associate Dean (Education) at the assessment design stage.

Under SCU Assessment, Teaching and Learning Policy (Section 3, Part A: Assessment Principles), Assessment Principle 1: Assessment is designed for student learning, engagement and success:

> (6) Our assessment: d. Is appropriate in volume and workload, manageable for both students and staff.

SCU Guide to assessment volume: https://spark.scu.edu.au/kb/tl/assess/guide-to-assessment-volume

Some troubling suppositions underlie exams: that students shouldn't work together, that they can't be trusted, that memorisation and recall are crucial, and that there is only 'one go to get it right'. Generally, everyone has to sit down simultaneously to do the exam (difficult when education spans borders and time zones), and time limits are imposed (presumably those with slower handwriting are at a disadvantage). These are only some of the many factors that make exams a high-stress activity for staff and students.

Sally Brown and Kay Sambell (2020), using the term "compassionate assessment", advocate for inclusive, just, authentic and intellectually challenging assessments designed so students come out of it with something definitively positive in the affective domain rather than feeling reduced or diminished.

At SCU, our assessment practices are still evolving, with steps taken to eliminate exams unless specific external accreditation reasons are approved by the relevant associate dean (Education). Taking it one step further, the policy advocates for a maximum of three authentic assessment tasks "that are performance-based, practice-based; industry-relevant; work-integrated; project-based; self-reflective or dilemma-based". While we are not yet at a fully compassionate level, these policies have significantly improved our approach to assessment. Beyond the assessment itself, however, other forms of policy and procedural support contribute to a pedagogy of kindness in the realm of assessment.

Overwhelming students with unnecessarily large, onerous and time-consuming assessments is unkind. But how does one choose between setting (say) a 1000-word or a 5000-word report? In addition to limiting the number of assessments to three or fewer, SCU provides an assessment volume guide to support academics in their choices regarding assessments. It exhorts academics to consider, among other factors,

- the appropriate type and amount of discipline-specific work students need to produce or perform to demonstrate their mastery of the learning outcomes;
- expectations regarding the students' cognitive effort and skills required to complete the assessments appropriate to the year level of study for this unit;
- factoring in the time and effort required for students to understand the expectations of the assessment, including rubrics and exemplars; and
- time and cognitive effort students will need to adequately process assessment feedback/feedforward in order to apply the knowledge and skills to the next assessment.

Moderate and calibrate for a just approach to marking

Under SCU Assessment Moderation procedures:

> (6) For best practice moderation, the Unit Assessor should develop, implement and facilitate an ongoing calibration process for all academic staff involved in teaching and marking the Unit, including those from all locations and partner collaborations.

Some subjects have larger cohorts than can be managed by a single academic. In those cases, universities rely on teaching and marking teams, usually led by a subject convenor. Assessment tasks for our students predominantly elicit extended complex responses. The marking of these involves making qualitative judgements and then, typically, assigning a numerical score. The scores are applied linearly as incremental measurements. However, the increments are not equidistant from each other in terms of value. For example, the implications of the interval between 48% and 51% (fail vs. pass) differ significantly from the interval between 58% and 61% (pass vs. pass).

Given that marking is predominantly a qualitative exercise, how do we ensure that markers are 'on the same page'? Injustice is galling. Education and the ensuing measuring of student learning outcomes need to be fair. If it's not fair, it's unkind. A pedagogy of kindness emphasises respect, compassion, empathy and justice. Together, these build a sense of trust. Unfairness, by comparison, erodes trust. Ensuring students' assessment works are marked fairly is a large part of building and maintaining trust.

Typically, universities apply a moderation process after assessments are marked. However, there appear to be holes in this method, which involves mending the 'tapestry of assessment marking'. The process of post hoc assessment moderation, where teams aim for consensus on (a) matters of judgement, (b) what constitutes quality and (c) how quality can be represented, is questionable. Such moderation is a retrospective approach: a narrow quality review process (Gillis, 2023) rather than quality assurance. A concomitant consequence of consensus review by academic teams is associated with a high workload, as this activity is repeated for each subsequent assessment.

This is not to suggest that subjective judgements are unsubstantiated opinions: these can most assuredly be "soundly based, [and] consistently trustworthy" (Sadler, 2012, p. 14). Quality, however, is an abstract concept. Multiple criteria are involved in judging and reporting quality (sometimes in fixed sets, as in rubrics). For example, a student's work can be deemed outstanding but for reasons not listed in the criteria.

Therefore, determining grades that reflect student levels of achievement relies on peer agreement regarding the quality of the assessment design (responsible as it is for the raw evidence of achievement produced by the student) and the associated marking criteria communicated to the students. Ipso facto, academic discussion around the meaning and significance of quality and what is deemed to count as evidence, needs to come before the design of the assessment, the articulation of marking criteria and teaching approaches. Sadler suggests that "[w]hereas moderation relevant for a single assessment task is repeated for subsequent tasks, the ultimate objective is the development of 'calibrated' academics" (2012 p. 17) – resulting in a situation where academics can produce grades without the need for third-party confirmation.

Such an approach towards 'calibrated academics' has not only repercussions concerning the distribution of workload (particularly for casual staff) but also multiple benefits: a more robust, peer-reviewed curriculum approach taught by academics confident in not only their informed judgment but also that of their colleagues and, above all, transparency in academic standards for peers and students alike.

Enhancing, refining and supporting the academic rigour of quality assurance by using academic calibration conversations helps achieve comparability of standards (Sadler, 2012). Calibration also helps establish that learning tasks used are valid preparation for key learning outcomes in a subject or discipline

(Sefcik et al., 2017). Additionally, regular academic calibration conversations build staff capacity. Participating in calibration is of lasting benefit to academics' development as educators. In the longer term, such academic development will further enhance the quality of educational delivery and processes. This, in turn, will enhance student outcomes.

Support academics with educational technologies

Under SCU Assessment, Teaching and Learning Policy, Section 3 (Policy Statement)

> [T]he University supports the use of technology (including generative artificial intelligence technology) in teaching, assessment and learning …

Under SCU Assessment, Teaching and Learning Policy, Teaching and Learning Principle 3 (Learning is supported by a consistent teaching delivery approach across the University).

> (16) Our teaching is:
>
> a Learning-centred, consisting of a combination of self-access learning and class learning that provide equivalent learning experiences for all students, regardless of mode or location of study;
> b Delivered through self-access learning, which consists of on-demand, self-paced, media-rich, interactive and responsive modules that provide automated feedback to students.

There are multiple practical factors related to university-wide curriculum design and support, ultimately supporting a pedagogy of kindness. Supporting academics' wise and adept use of educational technologies contributes to the well-being of students as they negotiate through their degrees. Facilitating technologies to foster engaging and interactive learning experiences for students can improve comprehension and retention of the material, increase access for students with disabilities and other abilities, and tailor resources and content in keeping with students' diverse learning styles, abilities, and work–life balances. Getting the units ready online in time for term commencement is essential, but it can be challenging for academics.

SCU employs educational technology facilitators. These staff specialise in higher education pedagogies and blended learning and conduct one-on-one and group training and professional development. The technology facilitators support staff uplift and build capacity in teaching technologies, tools and platforms for implementing the Southern Cross Model. A particular focus is on supporting e-learning and online and blended learning, underpinned by pedagogically sound and evidence-based practices and adult learning principles to support staff efficacy, capability and engagement in teaching technologies. The technology facilitators support selecting technologies appropriate to educational objectives and requirements that best support student outcomes.

At the start of the change to SCU's new academic model, it was envisaged that technology facilitators would only be needed to transition learning models to the new platform. It has transpired, however, that technology facilitators' effectiveness and ongoing support are invaluable, as demonstrated by the proactive engagement and feedback from academics who rely on their assistance.

Overall, the wise and effective use of educational technologies promotes student-centred learning, inclusivity, flexibility and preparedness for the future. It demonstrates a commitment to providing students with the best possible educational experience, which is a kind and considerate approach to their needs and aspirations.

Reduce cognitive load and overwhelm

The Southern Cross Model Key Features

> The academic year is divided into 6 Terms. Each Term is delivered over 7 weeks, with 6 weeks of teaching and a 7th week in each Term which may be used for study, review and assessment. A 2-week break occurs between Terms.
>
> Full-time students enrol in a maximum of 2 units per Term. Students are not required to study in all 6 Terms. Typically, a full-time student will study four Terms and complete 8 units a year. This means there are fewer units and fewer assignments and exams for a student to juggle at one time.
>
> From: https://www.scu.edu.au/staff/
> teaching-and-learning/the-scu-model/

The Southern Cross Model uses a focused, immersive scheduling model involving a six-week term with a maximum enrolment of two units per term to help students deepen their disciplinary studies. This scheduling model is a form of block scheduling wherein students take a limited number of courses or engage in specific learning experiences intensely over a shorter duration, such as a few weeks or a single semester. Concentrating on a limited number of subjects simultaneously allows for a more focused and immersive learning experience, as it reduces cognitive load.

A benefit of such a model is that it reduces the mental effort required for frequent context switching. *Context switching* refers to shifting focus or attention from one task or topic to another. It involves disrupting concentration and cognitive flow and imposes a mental cost. Each time the context is switched, it takes time for the brain to refocus and adapt, which can result in increased mental fatigue and reduced efficiency. While some context switching is inevitable in life, feeling pulled in different directions can lead to feelings of overwhelm and a decreased sense of wellbeing.

Positive outcomes of the new Southern Cross Model: A testament to the pedagogy of kindness

Data gathered during the roll-out of the new curriculum is positive. Student success rates have risen from 69.6% in 2019 to 86.7% in 2023. The mean grade point average rose from 3.65 (2019) to 4.52 (2023). Concomitantly, absent fail rates dropped (5.4% > 3%), as did 'early withdrawn' rates (13.7% > 6.5%). The SCU College, offering a range of preparatory pathway programmes for undergraduate and postgraduate studies, was the first faculty at SCU to wholly complete the staged transition to the new model and achieved highly significant improvement in success rates (Goode et al., 2022). Enabling programmes such as these traditionally experience high attrition rates (approaching 50%). In the summer term of 2023, SCU College successfully delivered all units in the new model, achieving an average 85% success rate and 92.8% student satisfaction.

Opening a world of possibilities: engaging and empowering students

As an exemplar of kindness within curriculum design, here is a practical example that showcases active learning and assessment within the SCU context. Through the Australian government's New Colombo Program (NCP) grants, academics are afforded the opportunity to provide students with a fully funded international study tour experience. In this context, I, Mieke, orchestrated and guided multiple two-week study tours in Singapore for students enrolled in a foundational first-year core subject. I targeted student equity groups (Indigenous, First in Family, low socio-economic status and LGBTI) across all campuses and online. The project aimed to build student expertise in intercultural business communication, promote student awareness and respect for cultural diversity, and raise awareness of international opportunities regarding networking and employment. The project was geared to empower and building student wellbeing, lifelong learning capacity and confidence.

The students engaged in the subject during the term but did not undertake the final assessment. Upon completion of the term, the students visited Singapore for two weeks, where they visited organisations and conducted research interviews with industry leaders to complete two assessment activities: a recorded conversation with an industry leader and researched reports worth 60% of their grade. Companies were offered the research consultancy reports created as a result. Cultural and language training enhanced the programme, as did a cross-institutional educational collaboration day with a Singaporean university.

The NCP Singapore study tour was a hugely beneficial experiential learning activity that improved my cultural understanding and provided networking opportunities as well as adding new perspective to the career goals I aim to achieve. The NCP trip has been the highlight of my time at university, and certainly the most valuable experience in terms of personal and professional development.

Unpacking this initiative illustrates elements of curriculum design that facilitate a pedagogy of kindness:

- a broad arena for designing and implementing authentic assessment design;
- experiential, active learning;
- industry relevance; and
- very practically, the flexibility to offer students extended incompletes.

The NCP study tours are an example of inspirational, transformative learning embedded within kindly structured educational policies, which enable individual agencies to enact kindness in a powerful way.

Conclusion

In decrying the 'structures of carelessness' in higher education, Clegg and Rowland (2010, p. 733) noted that

> [i]t would be possible, however, to look at how the organisation designs its systems, designs its buildings, places people, how it rewards or disparages activities and so on, and to ask whether seen through the lens of kindness these are likely to increase or decrease the possibility of kindness towards other people: students, colleagues across the boundaries of job descriptions, visitors.

We contend that as course and curriculum designers, we have a unique opportunity to look through that 'lens of kindness' as we deliberate, negotiate and establish 'what matters' and foreground what is relevant.

Without a focus on appropriate policies and procedures supporting course design, academics can, at best, practise kindness – by doing kind things and behaving in a kind way. Dall'Alba (2005) contends that a focus solely on the epistemology of teaching, or the act of doing teaching, fails to capture the essence of 'being' a teacher, thus limiting the potential for universities to fulfil their expected role and objectives (pp. 362–363). Our point here is that in order to go beyond surface-level acts of kindness and truly embody kindness as a fundamental aspect of teaching, it is essential to have pedagogically kind policies and procedures supporting course design. By embedding a pedagogy of kindness structurally within the design process, educators can cultivate a deeper level of kindness that transcends mere actions and enables a genuine state of being kind.

References

Biggs, J. (1999). Teaching for quality learning at university: What the student does. *Society for Research into Higher Education*. Open University Press.

Biggs, J., & Tang, C. (2011). *Teaching for quality learning at university*. Open University Press.

Brown, S., & Sambell, K. (2020). *Fifty tips for replacements for time-constrained, invigilated on-site exams*. Retrieved from https://teachlearn.leedsbeckett.ac.uk/-/media/files/clt/ftld2kay-sambellsally-brown-coronavirus-contingency-suggestions-for-replacing-onsite-exams-1.pdf

Clegg, S., & Rowland, S. (2010). Kindness in pedagogical practice and academic life. *British Journal of Sociology of Education, 31*(6), 719–735. https://doi.org/10.1080/01425692.2010.515102

Csikszentmihalyi, M. (1990). *Flow: The psychology of optimal experience* (1st ed.). Harper Collins. ISBN 9780061339202.

Dall'Alba, G. (2005). Improving teaching: Enhancing ways of being university teachers. *Higher Education Research and Development, 24*(4), 361–372.

Freeman, S., Eddy, S. L., McDonough, M., & Wenderoth, M. P. (2014). Active learning increases student performance in science, engineering, and mathematics. *Proceedings of the National Academy of Sciences, 111*(23), 8410–8415. https://doi.org/10.1073/pnas.1319030111

Gillis, S. (2023). Ensuring comparability of qualifications through moderation: Implications for Australia's VET sector. *Journal of Vocational Education & Training, 75*(2), 349–371. https://doi.org/10.1080/13636820.2020.1860116

Goode, E., Syme, S., & Nieuwoudt, J. E. (2022). The impact of immersive scheduling on student learning and success in an Australian pathways program. *Innovations in Education and Teaching International*. https://doi.org/10.1080/14703297.2022.2157304

Malti, T. (2021) Kindness: A perspective from developmental psychology. *European Journal of Developmental Psychology, 18*(5), 629–657. https://doi.org/10.1080/17405629.2020.1837617

Rust, C., O'Donovan, B., & Price, M. (2005). A social constructivist assessment process model: How the research literature shows us this could be best practice. *Assessment & Evaluation in Higher Education, 30*(3), 231–240. https://doi.org/10.1080/02602930500063819

Sadler, R. (2012). Assuring academic achievement standards: From moderation to calibration. *Assessment in Education: Principles, Policy & Practice, 20*(1), 5–19. https://doi.org/10.1080/0969594X.2012.714742

Sefcik, L., Bedford, S., Czech, P., Smith, J., & Yorke, J. (2017). Embedding external referencing of standards into higher education: Collaborative relationships are the key. *Assessment & Evaluation in Higher Education*. https://doi.org/10.1080/02602938.2017.1278584

Vervaeke, J., & Ferraro, L. (2013). *Relevance, meaning and the cognitive science of wisdom*. https://doi.org/10.1007/978-94-007-7987-7_2

Vervaeke, J., Lillicrap, T. P., & Richards, B. A. (2012). Relevance realisation and the emerging framework in cognitive science. *Journal of Logic and Computation, 22*(1), 79–99. https://doi.org/10.1093/logcom/exp067

Chapter 3

Kindness in assessment

Jo Munn and Rachel Matthews

Introduction

Assessment is central to teaching and learning and is also its most fraught aspect. It's critical and contentious because it is here that the 'rubber hits the road' and we get to see how the students have engaged and what they have taken on board. This aspect of teaching quickly becomes swampy: plagiarism, artificial intelligence (AI), over-assessment, scheduling, marking and institutional expectations all have an impact on both teachers and students. We have seen assessments scheduled for New Year's Day and heard many students' complaints about (the lack of) fairness and clarity and academics' concerns about integrity. We recognise the struggle to find a manageable balance between institutional policy, student expectations, and educators' own philosophy about assessment practices. We believe intelligent, authentic, and considered assessment design and practice sits at the heart of a pedagogy of kindness (PoK). This chapter contains two case studies. In the first, Jo Munn explores how a PoK can be applied to a challenge facing assessment integrity and rigour – generative AI (GenAI). In the second, Rachel Matthews describes her thinking and experience of designing a personalised and authentic assessment task that draws on a philosophical commitment to kindness and what that means for her wider practice.

Dancing with the tiger: Assessment and GenAI

Jo Munn

As an academic in a centralised centre for teaching and learning and at a regional university, I work with faculty academics to develop student-centred curricula with a core focus on assessment design. I work predominantly with health colleagues, due to my earlier disciplinary background. I did not know it then, but core to my teaching approach was a PoK. Central to my practice was being kind, empathetic and caring, fostered by encouraging a growth mindset

DOI: 10.4324/9781003364887-3

in students with whom I shared learning and teaching experiences. I worked to establish clear expectations for students, allowing them to feel safe to ask questions and see my vulnerabilities as a new academic, not claiming to know everything but modelling the importance of lifelong learning and ongoing reflective inquiry. Important was establishing a space of equal respect, with different skill sets, knowledge and experience all in one 'classroom'. Today, in my academic practice, I still try to interweave this approach with other pedagogies, but now, I realise this approach has a name, a PoK. Not only do I try to support academics to embed principles of kindness into the curriculum, but my approach to academics is also one centred on kindness, through empathy, compassion and care and recognising personal, institutional and sector pressures.

The following explores how we can apply a PoK to a challenge facing assessment integrity and rigour in the education sector, GenAI. I use practice examples, applying the principle of kindness pedagogy to using GenAI technologies in student assessment.

GenAI refers to AI models and algorithms designed to generate new content (Chan & Hu, 2023), including text, images, videos, music and code. Whilst I recognise student assessments will utilise many formats, the focus of this discussion will be written forms of language-based outputs. Language response models are a GenAI type designed to generate human-like responses in natural language. These models are trained on large-scale online data sets, enabling them to create contextually relevant text responses (Chan & Hu, 2023), for example, OpenAI's GPT (Generative Pre-trained Transformer) ChatGPT and Elicit.

The emergence of technology to support students in assessment is not new. The calculator analogy is frequently used to compare the emergence of GenAI. The introduction of the calculator generated initial resistance in education through fear that numeracy skills would regress. As the benefits were realised, educators shifted to understanding that the effective operation of calculators was integral to teaching mathematics and science (Rudolph et al., 2023).

Technologies have emerged that support student writing and information searching, from basic spelling and grammar checkers to more advanced third-party plugins such as Grammarly, originality checking tools to help refine paraphrasing, online language conversion tools and AI-integrated database searching tools. Technological advances make many 'academic' tasks easier and allow a focus on more complex, humanised skills like critical thinking, problem-solving and collaboration.

So, how does kindness fit in? If we apply a lens of kindness to designing assessments where GenAI is rapidly becoming part of the workplace, what does that look like? How do we strike a balance between ensuring academic rigour and integrity and doing right by our students to support them in developing capabilities in the ethical and critical use of GenAI, relevant to their discipline and future professional roles?

The notion of kindness is tied to fostering student skill development for employability (Rudolph et al., 2023) from a position of trust, care, and responsibility (Gorny-Wegrzyn & Perry, 2021) rather than adopting a punitive and prohibitive approach to GenAI use. It recognises how GenAI can be useful and by adopting its use in assessments in authentic ways, the essential human elements required to use GenAI tools ethically and effectively can be emphasised. You can show care and empathy by understanding how GenAI is used in real-world scenarios and provide your expectations around use to help build capabilities for its ethical and effective use from a position of mutual trust. Essentially, digital literacy education is critical and given the status quo, AI tools should be included in the curriculum (Rudolph et al., 2023).

Information literacy and critical thinking have long been core outcomes for students in higher education (White, 2021). As with any source of information, students need skills to search, appraise and acknowledge this information and find other credible evidence to support it. The introduction of GenAI allows access to focused information almost instantly. This can be streamlined through skilful prompt engineering to create outputs suitable for various contexts. As is with developing skills for traditional information and digital literacies, there is an opportunity to develop AI literacies (Long & Magerko, 2020), including skills for prompt engineering and critical judgements around GenAI outputs through assessment design. As a point on kindness, we are not doing things differently, just adapting to the ever-changing digital world, empathising with students, showing care that we recognise the reality, and applying core principles of digital and information literacy skills in an evolved context.

Our institution has adopted a liberal approach to GenAI, not prohibiting its use in assessment. Instead, academics are directed to provide clear guidance and expectations on the limits for acceptable and ethical use of GenAI suitable to the assessments and provide education around this. As I consult with academics, there is still understandable apprehension around wanting to allow students to use GenAI. Academics report that use may threaten the rigour of the assessment task and student learning of fundamental concepts and skills. Understandably, such hesitancy exists. I frame my consultancy conversations using some of the guiding ideas explored earlier. Key points that align with a PoK are that, as educators, we need to be responsible for building student capability for the ethical use of these tools. We can model and provide opportunities for practising the use of GenAI through the design of assessments, which challenge students to recognise the capabilities and limitations and how they think and process humans and can add value to outputs from AI. It comes from a place of understanding and care, the need to develop skills that connect with real-world expectations and one of trust and mutual respect, sharing how both students and teachers alike can use these tools to support productivity, but understanding the need for human scrutiny and developing the skills to use these tools ethically and effectively.

With the recognition of the potential value of letting students use available technology tools in ethical and responsible ways, the next questions I am asked in my consultancy are: What do you think would be acceptable limits to set for ethical GenAI use in this task? And Will gen AI be able to do the task and pass?

As a recent example, I worked with an academic in a tertiary education preparation programme. The connection here to how GenAI may be used in professional or industry-based practice may not be as relevant as for other disciplinary degree programmes. Still, as a launching pad for future successful academic studies, the academic realised the need for developing literacy skills and ethical use of such technologies that will be available for prospective study. There were three discrete assessment tasks for the unit. The core themes of the three assessments were time management, study planning, understanding one's strengths and weaknesses as a learner, self-reflection and identifying future approaches for effective learning. Needing to strike a balance between the opportunity to use GenAI responsibly and ethically and ensuring assessment rigour, a review of the assessments identified that assessment requirements were quite general and the likelihood of GenAI being able to generate a sound and adequate response for some components of the assessment tasks was high. As a result of further discussion, the academic adapted the assessments by focusing on asking students to contextualise their responses more explicitly.

The modifications required students to draw on specific examples in their preparatory programme related to the unique nature of study in our institution's intensive delivery model, both in reflection and in projection for how they would apply study skills in this specific course in the future. They were also asked to utilise course materials and support ideas with reference to the scholarly sources from the unit. The instructions set explicit limits to what was acceptable to seek GenAI input on and what was not, providing a statement that was not punitive in tone but guiding the identification of the importance of self-reflection to target one's own learning needs as a student, with the messaging coming from a position of trust and care.

Overall, the assessment briefs for each task clearly communicated guidelines for what was acceptable (and not) in a kind and caring way yet set clear boundaries and expectations for what was acceptable use.

In addition, the academic and I discussed learning moments that could be provided in class for using GenAI, extensions on critical thinking and accessing scholarly sources to support potential GenAI-generated ideas. We discussed that there could be opportunities for the teacher to model usage and student ideas sharing around how they might use it, its limitations, what would consti-tute ethical and appropriate use, and what checks and balances should be implemented. These learning opportunities were deemed necessary to support students' understanding and application of appropriate and ethical use of the tool for the summative tasks.

Let's not forget the academics and kindness to oneself. In a hectic work world, often, time is not on our side. We can embrace GenAI to help produc-tivity and support our teaching and assessment. Two core practice examples from a health-based assessment consultation involve establishing case studies and assisting with writer's block associated with establishing grade descriptors for a rubric. Generating 20 brief case scenarios for a practical/viva exam in an allied health discipline can take a lot of time. Implementing a few prompts into a GenAI tool and setting some parameters to streamline the content output for the discipline, such as the type of clinical problems, health assessments and interventions, the machine rapidly generated 20 draft case study briefs. Were they up to standard for the assessment task? No. But this is where the academic expert comes in. Using their human critical thinking skills and disciplinary expertise, the academic refined the prompts to improve the outputs and then tweaked each case study to provide any extra information to ensure alignment for the assessment.

As a next step, we call on our GenAI tool to help write grade descriptors across five grade bands. We ask the tool to generate these based on two differ-ent criteria: communication and clinical reasoning. Within seconds, we have 10 descriptors that need only minor tweaking to ensure alignment with our task and learning outcomes. The amount we achieved in engaging the GenAI tool in a 1-hour assessment design consultation was impressive. It certainly improved our productivity. The tool itself could not achieve the standard we required. It served as a starting point, and with the disciplinary and pedagog-ical expertise and critical thinking skills of humans, our job was a little easier, providing time efficiencies and kindness to self through what was achieved so rapidly.

As academics in higher education, we need to foster students' capabilities in using available technology, paralleling what is available in the real world. Digital literacies are rapidly changing and easy access to AI requires us to rec-ognise and support students' use of such tools. I believe in taking a kindness approach to assessment design that does not prohibit GenAI but instead incorporates expectations and models ethical and effective use. This way for-ward shows care and ensures students are equipped to use GenAI in appropri-ate ways, including outside university settings. This use does not comprise academic standards but rather embraces opportunities for productivity to allow more time for uniquely human skills. A PoK is founded on trust – that academics believe students and believe in them (Denial, 2019). We can enact PoK by modelling the effective and ethical use of GenAI in university assess-ment and beyond.

What's in your wardrobe? Kindness and practicality in assessment

Rachel Matthews

Introduction

I am Head of School for Design in a teaching institution that focuses on undergraduate courses in the creative industries. Prior to entering higher education, I worked as a designer in the UK and internationally. For a number of years, I worked across both the industry and education, with a passion for facilitating live projects in the courses I ran.

After deciding to commit to a career in higher education, I undertook a PhD investigating contemporary fashion taste-making practices in digital communications in the early twenty-first century. Through my research, I became fully immersed in narratives and counter-narratives of fashion trends and changes. This informed my research on taste-making and influence for my PhD; however, it also left me with a growing sense of unease and alarm about the direction of mainstream fashion, especially its negative environmental and social impacts.

Once I completed my PhD, I took a role running a fashion marketing programme at my current place of work. Based on the success of this programme I was asked to develop a fashion design programme that could complement and enhance existing fashion courses. Although I was still a passionate believer in design education, I felt conflicted by this request as I was growing more and more uncomfortable with the idea of promoting career paths in an increasingly problematic fashion industry. This discomfort was further compounded by a personal sense of guilt at my active participation in an industry that now appeared to be causing such issues.

After a period of professional discomfort and confusion, I found a solution to my inner conflict. I proposed a Bachelor of Design (Fashion & Sustainability) and undertook the task of finding a way to 'do' fashion education differently, to address the problems I had recognised in the fashion industry. In developing this new programme of study, I realised I would need to let go of certain 'old ways' (handed-down educational traditions) in fashion design that fuelled some of the issues apparent in the industry. 'Old ways' would need to be replaced in order to productively harness a designer's creativity for an era of environmental and social precarity; in particular, assessments would need to help change behaviours rather than only be a vehicle for students to demonstrate knowledge about sustainability (Fletcher & Williams, 2013).

Resetting attitudes/mindsets

I feel strongly that designers have a social responsibility to draw on personal values such as compassion, respect, and empathy towards people and resources as part of design decision-making. As I began developing the Fashion & Sustainability programme, I realised these values had not been seen as relevant in fashion education previously. This forced me to consider ways of designing the course to provide opportunities for students to identify and examine their attitudes and mindsets.

Furthermore, the purpose of fashion education has traditionally been framed in relation to 'the industry' and its needs. I wanted this new programme to position designers and their work more holistically, beyond just fashion situated in society and address society's needs (McArthur, 2022).

With these rather lofty ambitions for the new Fashion & Sustainability programme, I also began to see why being kind and compassionate was important for a course of this nature: investigating fashion's environmental and social impact could feel daunting and overwhelming for students. Asking students to undertake challenging work that draws on personal beliefs and values could evoke feelings of vulnerability and eco-anxiety and I felt I needed to create a caring, optimistic learning context without compromising criticality.

I wanted the course to offer a sense of hope and potential pathways to solving these issues and to focus on supporting young creatives to engage constructively with these complex problems. In seeking suitable theoretical framing for this area of study, certain critical pedagogies seemed relevant to support learners to question the status quo and their own attitudes and mindsets and help them effect change individually and in society. My understanding of the PoK evolved through designing and implementing the fashion and sustainability course. Inviting students to investigate 'big' existential issues comes with responsibility: a duty of care to provide a consistent and supportive environment in which to engage. Furthermore, being creative has always required a degree of courage, and finding creative solutions to some of the twenty-first century's most complex problems takes even greater courage. Adopting teaching strategies that promote an environment of trust and support amongst staff and students helps create spaces and opportunities to be brave in the face of things that at first appear difficult.

Assessment

The assessment design in Stage 1 of the fashion and sustainability course focuses on students' personal preferences and fashion behaviours. The assessments are designed to promote behaviour change and ask students to examine their personal relationships with fashion. In a unit called Fashion Design: Function, students undertake a personal wardrobe audit before using their findings to design a capsule wardrobe for themselves. The task requires students to review, categorise, and analyse the content of their own wardrobe and then present their findings to the group. At the presentation, students identify any patterns/habits they observe in their choices, reflect on what they see as their 'wardrobe essentials' and conclude by identifying their three favourite pieces (and a supporting rationale). In doing so, students begin to understand their own wardrobe behaviours and the various functions of fashion and clothing in their lives.

Although this activity appears technical, the findings can be personally confronting for students. They are often shocked by the sheer number of garments they own, often with large amounts of the same item such as jeans, hoodies and floral summer dresses, most of which are identical apart from small design differences. Other uncomfortable findings from the audit are around items that are unworn/worn only once. Interestingly, when students are asked to identify their three favourite pieces, these are not the garments worn the most but those with emotional connection or memories. The wardrobe audit task intends to challenge students in a positive and personally meaningful way. However, this requires students to expose aspects of themselves that usually remain hidden from view, with wardrobe items only seen in public when outfits have been carefully edited.

I introduce the assessment by giving a clear rationale: collectively, we are creating knowledge of wardrobe behaviours; everyone has something to contribute to this, and different experiences and preferences are important and provide us with depth in understanding fashion consumption. I am very clear about the marking criteria: there is no judgement being made about what is in people's closets! It is not about proving how sustainable you and your wardrobe items are or about designer name-dropping. Assessment criteria are based on data collection (the number of garments and their quality), data analysis, evidence of self-reflection, clarity of report and communication in the verbal presentation. It is possible to get a High Distinction in this project whether you have 5 or 505 items in your wardrobe.

I use the briefing and discussion of assessment criteria to set the tone for how I hope people will engage with this project. At the start of this assignment, students usually find the idea of using their own wardrobe compelling, chatting animatedly amongst themselves. I sometimes also sense that the group presentation for which students are required to share their findings (e.g. wardrobe contents) feels daunting, with students needing additional support/reassurance about this prospect. I have considered removing the group presentation and instead asking the students to do the audit and collate the findings and reflections in a report because of the concern it was causing. However, I decided to leave the presentation in the assignment, as so much of the learning here is in each person getting a better understanding of other ways people use fashion (and its diverse functions in different lived experiences).

PoK in practice

Recognising the pressure that some students feel around the group presentation, I decided to make this more interactive, pairing students up so it would run more like a Q&A session. I set a series of questions that everyone must ask their partners and then allow them to add three of their own questions. I also make it clear that no one has to share anything about themselves and their wardrobe contents that they aren't comfortable with (and underwear isn't included in the wardrobe audit!).

The students are paired up well in advance of the presentation, so they have time to get to know each other. As with most group work, some students work well together; others, not so much; however, the switch to the Q&A-type interview rather than a formal presentation diffuses the anxiety around sharing. To help students make progress on the audit assignment, each week in class, we all share one insight gained from examining the content of our wardrobes – me included. I start the discussion; sometimes we discuss observations around colour palettes or pattern preferences in our closets, or we talk about the oldest item we own. This helps students incrementally build up to the sharing experience required at the presentation and helps start conversations between students about their emotional connections to clothing and ideas of personal identity captured in clothing, as well as various histories of handed-down garments emerge. These informal conversations sometimes feel more valuable in learning how garments function in people's lives than the assignment, they prompt genuine interactions between students. There are always some students who do more talking than listening in these conversations, and I'm mindful of not creating an environment where just confident people are heard. It sometimes takes a few weeks, but everyone has something to share as they begin to develop curiosity in their own relationship with fashion and the wardrobes of others.

Generally, the presentation sessions run smoothly. Some students make new purchases to enhance their findings or use the presentation to demonstrate styling expertise. Although this can annoy some in the group, I note these as further insights on consumption practices, personal differences in self-fashioning preferences ... more collective knowledge sharing on how fashion functions in people's lives. At this point in the unit, I'm keen to see how students are responding to each other, such as what types of questions they ask each other and emerging friendship groups as this first part of the assessment tasks can act as a shared experience. I linger before and after my classes, listening and throwing in the odd conversation starter with the group. For me, it is important to gauge the level of trust and how successful my relationship-building endeavours have been so far. I do this in preparation for the second part of this assignment as it is usually quite challenging for students – using their findings to design a capsule wardrobe for themselves.

A student's drive to study fashion design can sometimes be underpinned and influenced by trend-driven runway fashion, where designers create highly conceptual ideas on the body for dramatic effect. So the notion of using their own wardrobe as a site of investigation to produce a collection for everyday wear can seem somewhat mundane, with some in the group finding it difficult to see themselves (and their wardrobe) as a source of inspiration. This situation requires me to create a space in which to be brave. For me, this means having a tough conversation with students, one during which I have to dismantle certain preconceptions/expectations about fashion and explain how the creativity of the designer now needs to be redirected to solve different sorts of problems. I often talk about my own disillusionment when I became aware of the negative impacts of fashion (after a 15-year career in the industry), as well as how I have found ways to shift my perspective to see a different future for fashion. I share examples of behaviour change in my personal life as well as highlight designers/brands who have inspired me by carving out new ways of 'doing' fashion.

I invite the group to talk about their motivations to study fashion and sustainability (rather than purely fashion design) – at this point, the conversation usually becomes even tougher, with issues of landfill, textile waste, plastic pollution and human rights abuse in the fashion supply chain ... it's the really ugly stuff that has informed their decisions. This honest discussion is hard and not everyone is prepared to engage; however, I use the low point of our shared dismay in fashion as a call to action for my students. The assessment task becomes a conduit for action, with momentum built on our sense of collective purpose. I echo Denial's (2019) sentiment: I see my students as collaborators and I believe that they can find new/other ways to 'do' fashion for sustainability; enacting a PoK helps me create a learning context in which they feel supported and able to try. Rebuilding excitement and curiosity about fashion after these tough conversations can take time. For me, PoK also means being patient and consistent, allowing students time to process our critical discussions and consider how to move forward. I know I need to turn up every week, prepared to revisit the tough conversation, listen to student ideas emerge on how they want to tackle issues and, from there, and create what Brown (2018) describes as a courageous culture – an environment to try something difficult as well as to give and receive feedback.

There are challenges and benefits of adopting a PoK; I have found it requires a delicate balance of compassion and courage, this balance is impossible to predetermine as it is affected by so many variables in the teaching context. Assessment design, underpinned by a compassionate outlook, can help by planning/engineering moments of human connection. Classes then become not simply about passing the assessment but can evolve a sense of community built around assessment as a shared experience. Assignment briefings can also be an important way for students to make connections, beyond social connections. Briefings are a chance to explain why the assessment matters in the context of the course and the context of work and society; this starts conversations with students about their individual creative and career goals. I can then frame assessment tasks as pit stops on their personal learning journey rather than the main purpose of study.

Enacting a PoK takes patience and time, sometimes a long time – and this can be challenging. It takes stamina to turn up with energy, optimism and purpose; plus, the impact of adopting a PoK is not always evident in assessment submissions, grades, or even graduate outcomes. However, I feel this approach does allow me to be more present with students, connecting with them as individuals and their learning rather than just getting them through my subjects. I think of the benefits of adopting PoK as ripple effects. Students in my classes witness my consistent compassionate approach, they see that I am empathetic and fair; this hopefully makes me approachable, enabling our interactions to be easy. This ripples out promoting an atmosphere of camaraderie in class that helps foster conversations between students, a solid base from which to build trust and engagement. Like ripples, however, the effects can also get obscured and distorted by competing demands!

I began this journey by recognising a need for more respect and compassion within the fashion industry. I sought ways to integrate these elements in fashion education and enact them in my teaching practice. The journey has prompted much personal reflection forcing me to consider how personal values such as care and respect can feature in curriculum design and be made tangible in the classroom. PoK has helped me find ways to bridge the personal, emotional, and professional aspects needed for a compassionate and critical learning context.

References

Brown, B. (2018). *Clear is kind. Unclear is unkind.* Brene Brown. https://brenebrown.com/articles/2018/10/15/clear-is-kind-unclear-is-unkind/

Chan, C. K. Y., & Hu, W. (2023). Students' voices on Generative AI: Perceptions, benefits, and challenges in higher education. https://arxiv.org/abs/2305.00290

Denial, C. (2019). A pedagogy of kindness. *Hybrid Pedagogy.* https://hybridpedagogy.org/pedagogy-of-kindness/

Fletcher, K., & Williams, D. (2013). Fashion education in sustainability in practice. *Research Journal of Textile and Apparel, 17*(2), 81–88.

Gorny-Wegrzyn, E., & Perry, B. (2021). Exemplary educators who embrace a teaching philosophy guided by a pedagogy of kindness. *Journal of Advances in Education Research, 6*(2), 67–74. https://doi.org/10.22606/jaer.2021.62002

Long, D., & Magerko, B. (2020, April 25–30). What is AI literacy? Competencies and design considerations. *2020 CHI Conference on Human Factors in Computing Systems*, Honolulu, Hi. USA. https://doi.org/10.1145/3313831.3376727

McArthur, J. (2022). Rethinking authentic assessment: Work, well-being, and society. *Higher Education, 85*(1), 85–101.

Rudolph, J., Tan, S., & Tan, S. (2023). ChatGPT: Bullshit spewer or the end of traditional assessment in higher education? *Journal of Applied Learning & Teaching, 6*(1). https://doi.org/10.37074/jalt.2023.6.1.9

White, A. M. J. (2021). Information literacy and critical thinking in higher education: Some considerations. In M. Khosrow-Pou (Ed.), *Research anthology on developing critical thinking skills in students* (pp. 111–124). IGI Global. https://doi.org/10.4018/978-1-7998-3022-1.ch007

Chapter 4

Deliberate design is kind design

Kelly Galvin

Moving into learning design was not where I expected to be after 15 years of being a health practitioner and academic teacher/clinical supervisor. Writing and developing curricula for face-to-face and online learning modes while teaching clinical skills helped me build an effective conceptual and practical toolkit for a learning designer. Being both a health practitioner and a teacher provided insight into how people think, learn, change and act over time and in situated contexts and aided me to shape a pragmatic approach to my worldview in general, which influenced how I searched for ways to understand 'what works' in learning design. This pragmatic approach inspired co-designing curricula with stakeholders in various higher education institutions in Australia and the UK (Galvin & Bishop, 2011).

I used design-based research (DBR) to explore ways of enhancing undergraduate health science students' clinical reasoning development in my doctoral research which I undertook while employed as a senior learning experience designer. This helped me develop an understanding that learning design is enriched when it has a foundation in kindness. The notion of kindness in learning design is one that evolved while working with stakeholders on new subject developments and when updating existing subject materials. Typically, these projects involved working closely with an academic subject matter expert (SME).

This chapter begins with the story of Jack, a health science academic, whom I worked with to introduce problem-based learning in an undergraduate health science subject. It illustrates how deliberately using kindness as an approach to learning design can be effective for teachers and students.

What happened at the end – The outcome of the learning design process

There was an unusual flurry of activity happening in Jack's online class when I entered as a guest. I wasn't used to students turning up to a non-mandatory online class in the final week of trimester, especially when assignments had already been submitted.

DOI: 10.4324/9781003364887-4

'Welcome Kelly', Jack wrote in the chat.

He announced I was the learning designer responsible for creating the decision wheel tool students had utilised to build confidence in clinical decision-making (Galvin, 2022, 2023). I feared I was about to be met with a barrage of negative feedback from students. I turned on my camera and microphone, smiled and thanked Jack for inviting me. Why did Jack invite me? It had been six months since I'd joined Jack's class as a guest. He and I had been through a journey together over the past year and I thought the last thing he'd want was to invite more dialogue with me now that he was officially free of our subject redevelopment.

'We wanted you to see what a difference the decision wheel tool has made to our class this trimester', Jack said warmly. A series of thumbs up, clapping hands and love hearts sprang up in the chat. I was surprised by the students' response.

Jack's subject was one that had a history of being incredibly problematic. It was a first-year undergraduate cross-disciplinary health science subject in which students needed to develop confidence in applying the foundations of clinical case taking, a skill which often left many feeling overwhelmed. Students, individually and in groups, worked through the basics of conceptually unpacking case studies and practised making decisions on how to prioritise case history questions, physical examinations and tests, or treatment management. I was aware that there had been a history of excessive cheating on tests, along with students choosing not to finish the practical clinical units. When these issues became too much for the faculty to ignore, I was assigned to work alongside Jack to give the subject an 'upgrade' by introducing a specific type of problem-based learning.

Jack, like many others in his field, toggled between his commitments as a practising health clinician and teacher. He once told me he viewed teaching as a way of gaining avenues to expand the clinical research activity.

'I never really wanted to be a teacher', Jack had often said to me. When I think back, there were days I pushed Jack a little too hard to get him to see inside the head of a learning designer. Interestingly, in the end, our success came after I changed tack by instead learning how to get inside Jack's head.

Thinking back to where we started, nothing matched with what I was seeing now. Jack was sharing an online forum with two columns, titled 'Individual decision wheels' and 'Group decision wheels'. He had asked the students to upload their individual decision wheels onto the online forum. The intention was that these completed first attempts would display up to eight filled-in wheel sections, each one colourfully reflecting their response to the question of what was most important in how their group had worked together and what challenges they faced during the trimester. Once this first individual decision wheel activity was complete, students moved into breakout rooms to answer the same questions, essentially to create small-group versions of the decision wheel to also upload and share.

Challenges your group has faced

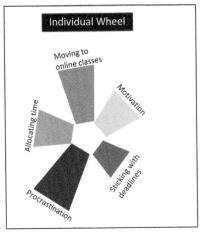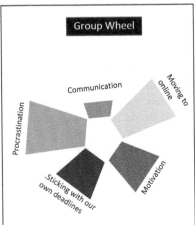

Figure 4.1 Individual and group decision wheel online class exercise.

Jack played gentle thinking music and live-streamed a video of baby otters at the local zoo in the upper corner of the screen. I was surprised at how calming this was.

Suddenly, the online forum began to populate with colourful individual and group decision wheels. My heart skipped a beat in excitement (Figure 4.1).

'Now, you're invited to turn on your microphone, or comment in the chat space, what these wheels tell us. Share with us if you're surprised by the comparison between individual and group wheel outputs.' Jack smiled again. I had never seen him smile quite like that in our dealings over the past year.

The students began to share, negotiate, respectfully discuss and reflect together. They did this, even though this class was not mandatory. Jack asked if they wanted to give me any specific feedback about their experience of the subject or of using the decision wheel tool.

A student immediately turned on her microphone:

> Every group discussion we had with the decision wheel highlighted items I had not yet considered. Group work makes me more accountable too, as it means it is harder to switch off. I need to pay more attention during group work. I am also motivated to fill in my decision wheels because my other group members are relying on me.

It wasn't what I was expecting to hear about group work from a student. Another student spoke up:

> We had a little bit of an argument using the decision wheel today and it kind of felt like a real discussion, about why we thought that was a

different priority. In the end we discussed it and we learned about the other person's perspective of why they think that was more important and less important.

Another student spoke:

I really liked how you could compact a lot of information into the decision wheel. I found it to be a great way to consolidate words to discuss things and to prioritise different important things.

There were comments of agreement in the chat.
Jack thanked them and added:

I think it's been a really good way to encourage you all to stay engaged and thinking about topics. Having the decision wheel seemed to help having to make decisions without that being too confronting. I noticed you were putting your opinions and your ideas down to share with others. There was not the same level of stress I often see that comes with speaking up in front of the class.

One student posted a lengthy chat message that prompted a huge amount of support from the group:

I agree Jack. I suffer with social anxiety and to have a tool to go, 'yep, okay, I'm really confident in this area', has made it easier for someone like me to speak up and feel like I'm not just being pushed aside by the rest of the group. I'm the sort of person that I will go one of two ways in a group, I will either do the entire thing myself, or if there is another dominant personality, I will shut up and do as I'm told. Having this tool helped me feel confident to have my say.

After the session, Jack asked me to stay online. He thanked me for helping him feel not only inspired to be a better teacher but also understand how to answer the 'what for?' question he had asked me so many times over the past year. I cast my mind back to our 1:1 meetings. 'What do I need to know about learning design for?' Jack had taken to asking me repeatedly during those sessions.

'Most of all, Kelly, I want to thank you for being kind. For me, using the decision wheel is one of those tools that is just going to get more effective the longer I teach it and embed it in certain teaching touch points.' Jack was very pleased with the improvements.

I left that online class realising that Jack and I had finally developed a mutual trust and respect and that he was right in saying it was kindness that helped us in the redevelopment of the subject (Denial, 2019; Perry et al., 2022). This began when we faced the initial question together: 'What can be done with this subject?'

The beginning of the learning design story – THEN

Conceptual learning design phase

'Hi, I'm Kelly and I'll be working with you as a learning designer to help reconsider how this subject could be enhanced for learners and to reduce pain points for learners and teachers.' I made this routine announcement in the online subject summit. In attendance were learning designers, media experts, discipline experts, language and library services support staff, a student representative and Jack, the lead academic assigned as the SME. He appeared unhappy to be there and to meet me.

There was a historical reliance on exams and case report assessment, the typical assessment types for health science subjects, both of which had alarming rates of cheating. The subject builds the foundation of clinical reasoning and decision-making, so cheating on assessments was extremely concerning for academics and potentially detrimental to patient health outcomes.

I shared my PhD research on merging elements of traditional problem-based learning with team-based learning to enhance clinical reasoning development to integrate teacher- and student-led approaches (Galvin, 2023). Jack still looked unimpressed. However, I pushed on with my pitch.

I showed an example of a simple decision wheel tool designed by the media team which could be used for both formative non-graded activities and as part of formal assessment to illustrate how students might be encouraged to think through ideas when making clinical decisions. I provided a link to the online tool for participants to practice with, inviting them to share their experience once they'd had a go. Pamela, from learning services, excitedly talked through her decision wheel attempt while sharing a colourful snapshot of her ideas for appropriate assessment types for this subject. She had rated each assessment idea in relation to relevance for first-year undergraduate students. Her example inspired others to add further ideas while enthusiastically showing their decision wheel attempts. Jack seemed even more unimpressed.

By the end of the meeting, just about everyone was excited about the possibilities. The one person I'd hoped would be on board was looking more disengaged and perplexed than ever. I asked Jack to stay online after everyone left.

'Jack, I get the feeling you're not convinced about how a PBL [problem-based learning] approach using an online decision wheel might be a way forward for this subject'. My directness seemed to help Jack feel comfortable to share his concerns.

Jack talked about feeling totally overwhelmed when listening to the myriad ideas for how the subject could be enhanced. He'd taken on the project thinking he only had to update the reading material and exam questions. It now seemed a huge amount of extra work for him in an area he was unfamiliar with and felt unprepared for, and he didn't know how to start. He had concerns about how to write for digital media assets and bigger concerns about the time implications required for learning new ways of writing content. In my mind, it had been clear that this new PBL approach and use of the online decision wheel not only fit the current research for this subject but also aligned perfectly with the institutional teaching and learning principles and objectives (Galvin, 2023; Torrens Global Education, 2021). However, I quickly realised that I needed to take time to learn more about how this new approach fit with Jack and his learners if I was ever going to attempt to challenge assumptions and the previous structure of the subject (Stephens, 2021). Jack and I agreed to meet weekly for the next six weeks.

My redesign process began by gathering as much student feedback on this subject as I could. It was obvious from the recordings I watched of previous online classes that students experienced a significant level of cognitive overload that hindered both learning and engagement.

This online subject used a flipped classroom design that the institution embedded into most subjects. This approach meant that students were expected to engage in content, housed in the learning management system (LMS), prior to attending a synchronous live class with their allocated teacher (Hew et al., 2021; Jia et al., 2021). Engagement is vital for this approach to be successful and it is important for teachers to have a strong online asynchronous presence before and after synchronous class time (Akçayır & Akçayır, 2018; Jia et al., 2021; Wanner & Palmer, 2015). I came to the conclusion that Jack's subject needed a complete overhaul.

I discovered through my benchmarking exercise of similar subjects that when students were provided with videos of character scenarios unfolding through real-life situations in clinical practice, they became 'hooked'. These case scenarios were useful when linked to online decision tree activities that students could use to practice making decisions and feel prepared for discussing ideas in a bigger group (Galvin, 2023; Garrett & Callear, 2001; Hai-Jew, 2014; Henshall et al., 2017; Mohan et al., 2017).

This appeared an ideal option for Jack's subject. I was feeling optimistic and ambitious after seeing these examples, but I did wonder if it was realistic to bring in this kind of innovation in the timeframe we had, especially as Jack was overwhelmed at the thought of reducing the number of readings.

When Jack and I met the next week, I shared my ideas. One assumption I came to this meeting with, was that offering students a range of activities would assist their learning and promote a more equal and accessible approach (Galvin, 2023). I had convinced myself early on that although support would be needed for this type of online PBL group learning, if designed well, there would also be plenty of opportunity for successful self-directed learning (Galvin, 2023). When my ideas made no dent in softening Jack's disengagement, I decided to stop doing all the talking (Denial, 2021; Stephens, 2021). I asked Jack what he was thinking.

'I don't care how best to design this subject, I'll teach it the way I want to anyway', Jack answered.

I cast my mind back to years of being a health practitioner. I decided that I had a duty of care to uphold at this moment for the subject, the learners and the teachers. In that moment, I decided to care about Jack and offer him the opportunity to feel more comfortable to exchange ideas (Denial, 2019, 2021; Perry et al., 2022; Rawle, 2021).

I wanted to better understand why Jack seemed so angry and he didn't hold back. He was frustrated because working on this project would take time away from research that he believed was far more important. And having to work with a learning designer was frustrating, because how could I ever possibly know what was expected from his discipline or know what was best for the students he knows so well. Even though I hadn't mentioned I was also a health practitioner, I did think he made a valid point. I could help him and this subject better if I understood the context of his experience with the subject matter more fully (Campbell, 2022; Rawle, 2021).

'If we're going to understand what can be done with this subject Jack, let's first discuss the learning outcomes, what you want students to know by the end of trimester, and how you want to assess evidence of their knowledge'.

Together, we drafted a list of six learning outcome examples to present to the wider group at our next development meeting. At that meeting, Jack reached a turning point when he saw key industry people and academic colleagues constructively engage in developing learning outcomes (Galvin, 2021).

In our next meeting, I broached options for integrating non-graded and graded formative digital learning activities into the subject. I was met with a familiar wave of resistance, so I decided to model the decision wheel tool I had shown earlier to the stakeholders (Perry et al., 2022; Rawle, 2021). Our question for this activity was, 'How might we best assess first-year undergraduate health students to perform clinical health assessments for a variety of cases?'

The first landing page of the decision wheel had space to add up to eight types of assessment. Jack quickly added an exam, a case report and a short-answer workbook as his ideal assessment types. I could sense he felt sure he'd covered all the bases. I added portfolio, role-play, group presentation, live brief and digital storytelling/reflection activity. Jack scoffed, but I moved on to the next landing page.

'Okay, Jack, because this is a group decision wheel, let's have a go at negotiating and deciding on how we would rate each of these ideas as most suitable for achieving the learning outcomes.'

'Not yet,' Jack blurted. 'I may as well have a go at filling out my own decision wheel first and then we can work on this one together.'

I was thrilled by this response as it appeared that Jack not only was engaged and wanted to have his own freedom of voice but was also motivated to exchange ideas (Perry et al., 2022).

After this session, Jack and I often used the decision wheel if we got to a point of tension. It helped us focus on the discussion rather than feel our comments were personal (Galvin, 2023). I found out later that Jack kept all his decision wheel attempts to help reflect on his own changes in thinking during the project.

Jack had reached a turning point in terms of understanding options for assessment and learning activities, but he was still overwhelmed by how it was going to work. It was more than giving him a checklist of ideas for how the subject could be improved (Rawle, 2021). He needed to know how to organise time and resources to ensure all the components could come together efficiently.

Practical learning design phase

To achieve a contextually relevant, constructively aligned, evidence-based design we set a clear writing plan that allowed time for research, innovation and feedback. The newly appointed project coordinator outlined workload timeframes and I could feel Jack shutting down when he realised he needed to complete the assessment briefs; develop new rubrics; re-package previous 'content' in various ways, including visual and audio formats; and decide on the reading material.

'I feel like I'm looking down the barrel of a black hole of time that's going to swallow me up very quickly', Jack said as he stared at the blank pages before him.

I showed Jack examples of case scenario templates from similar subjects along with activities I was hoping to introduce into this subject, which helped him find his feet somewhat. However, when I asked him to write digital media scripts for videos and online decision tree games, his anxiety peaked. I, by comparison, was excited that I'd negotiated extra pay in recognition of Jack's increased workload. In retrospect, this was a pivotal moment. I had clearly dropped the ball of tuning into Jack's optimal pace of working during the busy development cycle, so much so that I was surprised when sharing news of extra time and money for digital media writing wasn't well received.

'Jack, I've created a new template for you to fill in for this decision tree activity'. I'd emailed the template through the day before and now had it up on my screen. In my mind, it was simple. 'Jack, just write a case study, provide a few options, then write feedback on which option was optimal and why'. The next day, Jack copied some brief case scenarios into the template with 'yes' or 'no' answers, much like a simple multiple-choice questions, sent it to me, then began cancelling our 1:1 meetings. I was confused about why Jack had not understood the brief of his writing task.

Our plan outlined the deadlines for finalising the scripts and I became frustrated that Jack didn't seem to care about them. The pressure was building as the scripts had to be proofread by the editing team, which was ready to roll into the production phase. Eventually, Jack answered my call.

'You really are sticking to me like velcro, Kelly'.

'I have some news that may be a relief', I said. 'Will you attend a meeting with me and one of our digital media experts this week?' I heard Jack sigh. 'Instead of you completing the templates, we will ask questions and then fill in the gaps'.

'So, all I do is answer questions?' Jack asked and then hesitated. 'No more asking me to fill in this plethora of templates?'

Jack attended the meeting with our media designer, Jon. I watched as Jack began to show some passion again when Jon asked all the right questions to draw out what he needed for bringing a case scenario to life. During this one extended meeting, Jon gained what he needed from Jack and was able to deliver a script to the actors who were waiting to film a series of clinical situations.

The next day, as Jack talked, I filled in the decision tree template. We were now keeping to the plan and Jack seemed invested and engaged in the project. This was what was needed all along: less pressure on Jack to learn how to complete the scenario template and write in an unfamiliar style.

Jack reached all learning design milestones for the various teams and the subject was developed on time and on budget. It looked fabulous and I could tell Jack was excited and even proud of this new approach. As Jack needed help to guide students in how to use the materials, there was a budget for me to coach him and for both of us to better understand 'what works' for the students when engaging with the learning materials.

Reflexive learning design phase

It was during the four-week period leading up to census date (when students can withdraw without financial or academic penalty) that I met with Jack for an initial 'subject health check' meeting. The program manager indicated that initial student feedback had not been positive. She shared a string of emails from students who passionately expressed feelings of being overwhelmed and confused.

'The subject was "megalithic" so I did not have much time to engage with the material', was the first student email.

'Due to having so many learning activities in the subject, it became overwhelming and I am not sure how to link them all together', another student wrote.

The next two comments surprised me as we had provided instructional resources in reading and media format for students and teachers to learn how to use the tool.

The teacher should make a video showing how to use a decision wheel tool, instead of the learning designer. The teacher demonstrating the use of the wheel in the live class is best as everyone watches the recording then.

I mean, the lecturer talked a lot about doing these learning activities before class, but never actually took us through it, and potentially there would have been more connection to this style of learning had we gone through the activities in a lecture [typed in bold].

I reminded myself that it was early days and that, at the very least, the students were engaged enough to write feedback so early in the term. I met with my own manager and shared the disappointing news. My manager recommended that I take care of myself during this period of mentoring Jack during his first time delivering the subject (Campbell, 2022). I was surprised by that response, but my investment in the subject was refuelled when I was reminded that innovation is rarely perfect the first time around and that we had the opportunity to gather more student feedback so we can learn quickly to keep improving (Denial, 2019, 2021). Hearing this permission for change to be bumpy at first was an enormous relief and helped me consider how I could help Jack through this turbulent stage. I also reminded myself there was the possibility there were good student experiences.

To help determine what was working, I gathered information from a variety of sources: Jack and I met regularly to debrief; I attended a live class to observe the way Jack encouraged the PBL approach; I observed how engaged students were with the asynchronous environment; and I re-engaged with relevant literature. I gathered more insight into cognitive overload theory and Universal Design for Learning (UDL) strategies and noted accessibility needs for learning online (Ashman, 2021; de Araujo Guerra Grangeia et al., 2016; Galvin, 2023; Haji et al., 2015; Moffitt et al., 2020). Jack seemed to appreciate our conversations as they helped spark ideas for his teaching (Gorny-Wegrzyn & Perry, 2021).

Halfway through the first subject delivery, students asked for their own asynchronous online space to use without needing the teacher to open up live classes or record sessions for them. Over four weeks, students utilised this online space over 1000 times to engage autonomously, either for individual learning or in their assigned groups. Students also told us when they needed more synchronous drop-in sessions with Jack to guide them with group work. Jack was happy to trial this approach instead of delivering the timetabled 3-hour online classes. Students attended more drop-in sessions after this adjustment.

The program manager called me to a meeting in Week 11 and enthusiastically shared feedback from students.

The first comment was inspiring:

The decision wheel tool helped bring a reason for our team to come together for our group work task. I really enjoyed the whole concept of the wheel and the scenarios that were presented with it. When we used it together online, I felt like I was face-to-face in a class working together as a team and collaborating on the ideas.

Another student wrote:

I would have had a completely different outcome for my assessment if I had not used the wheel tool. It helped a lot to come to the best outcome because it helped me to notice ratings, priorities and things to consider. If I had not used the wheel, the considerations to reflect on would not have been as broad.

Jack had also provided feedback to the program manager and was happy for me to see his comments:

Because the decision wheel tool was the non-assessable aspect of the assessment, as the teacher I could see all the attempts were their own and not done by someone else. It is very exciting to be able to see all the incredible resources and ideas to support the development of this subject now. Compared to the way the subject was previously written, this is truly inspiring and I think the quality of the subject is the highest standard it has ever been.

I reflected on the effort the subject redevelopment had taken and how much we'd all learnt. The next question was, 'How could this continue to make a positive impact for the future?'

Evaluative learning design phase

After the first delivery the subject wouldn't run for three months, so there was time to evaluate the outcomes and feedback. I looked over my notes and was stunned at the number of assumptions I had made. One assumption was that it was the act of decision-making that needed to be the central focus for the subject to be successful (Galvin, 2023). At the conclusion, I reflected on the number of times we had to pivot our thinking to instead approach design principles from a far more holistic viewpoint now understood after taking time to hear from those experiencing the learning design (Galvin, 2023).

Key improvements included ensuring students and teachers would be able to edit decision ideas with more ease during a decision wheel tool attempt and providing more ways for teachers and designers to customise the set categories in the decision wheel tool to help early learners focus on negotiating ratings (Galvin, 2023). Additionally, we knew more about how learning was enhanced when teachers offered regular instructional videos and set synchronous touchpoints between teachers and learners to help navigate the PBL experience

(Galvin, 2023). Other design improvements listed included building online optional communal spaces for learners and offering regular coaching support to both the key teacher and the students throughout the trimester (Galvin, 2023).

I eagerly made another list of what ways I could promote sharing this scholarship of learning. First, I noted I would like to invite Jack to deliver a presentation with me on this for our next Learning and Teaching Symposium for the university and present an overview and granular findings from this project to our learning design team the following month.

It came back to me how often Jack had asked me, 'What do I need to do this for?' during this learning design project. I could hear Jack's voice in my head asking many questions, 'Kelly, what can we do with this subject?' 'What plan do you have for us?' 'What is working with this subject?' and, finally, after we met for the final time during his first delivery of the subject, 'What do we do now?'

It was when I was dutifully mowing the lawn one weekend that a process sequence began circling my mind to help answer Jack's questions. It was not lost on me that I must really love this job, as I am still thinking about it while being spat at by grass clippings.

The next day, I created an infographic to help express this perspective of learning design stages using a 'What Four' design plan (Figure 4.2).

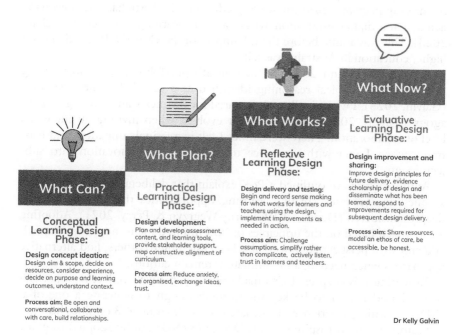

Figure 4.2 The 'What Four' learning design process (author).

Two weeks later, I was preparing once again for a new cycle of subject summits for new or redevelopment projects. I opened the online meeting and greeted our guests. As usual, I looked at the sea of faces in attendance, including learning designers, media experts, discipline experts, language and library services support staff and a student representative, all present for this new subject upgrade. There was also Natalie, the lead academic assigned as the subject matter expert to upgrade the subject. Natalie did not look even the slightest bit happy to be there, or to meet me. She opened up her microphone and said, 'What are we doing this re-development for?'

This time, I felt more confident and prepared for how to begin our learning design journey together. I piped up: 'That is a great question, Natalie'. The sea of faces looked at me a bit confused as they had pre-empted a terse response from me. 'Can I take the time to show you a model I've followed in the past that may help answer your question?' Natalie seemed open to hear what I had to say.

'I am going to answer your "what for?" question by explaining a "What Four" approach we can take during this project, together'. Just like that, the learning design journey began again.

Epilogue

In 2018, when I began my doctoral project, technology was ranked as one of the most important factors influencing education in Australia, with a growing demand for digital innovation to elevate the learning experience (Galvin, 2023). This was a time before the full impact of the COVID-19 pandemic on higher education in Australia was felt.

Between 2018 and 2022, 80 new health portfolio subjects were being developed with clinical reasoning identified as a key skill to be developed (Galvin, 2023). I was initially not prepared for the messy and 'entangled pedagogy' (Fawns, 2022) experience that evolved when inviting an increased level of collaboration. There were times I felt increasingly impatient and frustrated when I met with resistance to implementing innovation into subject design.

Authors who have outlined a PoK explain that deliberately designing with kindness incorporates creating learning opportunities that are robust and deeply considered (Denial, 2019; Gorny-Wegrzyn & Perry, 2021). Adopting an approach based on the principles of PoK inspired me to not only acknowledge my own perspectives but to also keep listening to others, find alternative approaches when needed, and, ultimately, remain curious.

In writing this chapter, I also made time to creatively reflect on what elements I understood to be key for learning design to generate a one-of-a-'KIND' learning experience in a situated context. Figure 4.3 outlines how key indicators of Knead Inspired Nexus Design (KIND) can be adopted to guide how deliberate learning design can be authentically KIND.

Knead

- Use time to shape ideas and plan a scaffold of learning experiences. Invite stakeholder feedback on learning design.
- Use insights from reflective activities to shape new ideas.
- Change and improve design ideas over iterative action cycles.

Inspired

- Learn from contextual and external creative and quality ideas to inform processes and use of learning design outcomes.
- Be driven by stakeholder contributions and current literature on design.
- Learn through taking risks and not fearing trying new design ideas.

Nexus

- Connect and collaborate with stakeholders using learning design.
- Bring designers, teachers and learners together to co-create learning design and let continuous improvement be informed by these relations.

Design

- Use design principles to build a deliberate alignment between learning outcomes, threshold learning concepts, and principles of a pedagogy of kindness (PoK) to build a 'One-of-a KIND' learning experience.

Figure 4.3 One of a 'KIND' learning experience (author).

It was exciting for me to consider the 'What Four' process as a way of integrating principles of DBR and a PoK that could be applied in any learning design project to also develop a 'one-of-a-KIND learning design'.

Conclusion

I have shared the concept of enacting a PoK when designing learning in this chapter with the use of a fictional case story based on several real-life scenarios.

The case story describes how, by deliberately adopting a PoK as a learning designer, I successfully worked with Jack to generate opportunities for transformational learning. The learning design process required me to build in time to hear Jack's perspective, negotiate ideas, understand what support he needed and be ready to change my approach, realising it isn't always about the academic needing to change.

This story is a tale of how the process of learning design can model kindness in learning in every sense by taking a deliberate approach with care. A tale worthy of telling, with kindness.

References

Akçayır, G., & Akçayır, M. (2018). The flipped classroom: A review of its advantages and challenges. *Computers & Education, 126*, 334–345. https://doi.org/10.1016/j.compedu.2018.07.021

Ashman, G. (2021, July 24). Universal design for learning (UDL) is the new learning styles. *Filling the pail.* https://fillingthepail.substack.com/p/universal-design-for-learning-udl

Campbell, C. (2022, May 9). Pedagogy of kindness for our exhausted academics: What can be done? *Ascilite TELall blog.* https://blog.ascilite.org/pedagogy-of-kindness-for-our-exhausted-academics-what-can-be-done/

de Araujo Guerra Grangeia, T., de Jorge, B., Franci, D., Martins Santos, T., Vellutini Setubal, M. S., Schweller, M., & de Carvalho-Filho, M. A. (2016). Cognitive load and self-determination theories applied to E-learning: Impact on students' participation and academic performance. *Plos One, 11*(3), e0152462. https://doi.org/10.1371/journal.pone.0152462

Denial, C. (2019, August 15). A pedagogy of kindness. *Hybrid Pedagogy.* https://hybridpedagogy.org/pedagogy-of-kindness/

Denial, C. (2021, January 29). Pedagogy of kindness [Video]. *YouTube.* https://www.youtube.com/watch?app=desktop&v=aaITtXvQM7U

Fawns, T. (2022). An entangled pedagogy: Looking beyond the pedagogy – Technology dichotomy. *Postdigital Science and Education.* https://doi.org/10.1007/s42438-022-00302-7

Galvin, K. (2021). *Learning outcome development toolkit.* Torrens University Australia (TUA).

Galvin, K. (2022). *The decision wheel tool.* http://x16.space/dw/

Galvin, K. (2023). *Clinical reasoning development: Enhancing independent and group rational decision making.* Torrens University Australia. https://torrens.figshare.com/authors/Kelly_Galvin/8628611

Galvin, K., & Bishop, M. (2011). *Case studies for complementary therapists: A collaborative approach.* Churchill Livingstone/Elsevier.

Garrett, B. M., & Callear, D. (2001). The value of intelligent multimedia simulation for teaching clinical decision-making skills. *Nurse Education Today, 21*(5), 382–390. https://doi.org/10.1054/nedt.2001.0568

Gorny-Wegrzyn, E., & Perry, B. (2021). Inspiring educators and a pedagogy of kindness: A reflective essay. *Creative Education, 12*(1), 1. https://doi.org/10.4236/ce.2021.121017

Hai-Jew, S. (2014). Branching logic in the design of online learning: A partial typology. *Packaging digital information for enhanced learning and analysis: Data visualization, spatialization, and multidimensionality,* 47–69. https://doi.org/10.4018/978-1-4666-4462-5.ch003

Haji, F. A., Khan, R., Regehr, G., Drake, J., de Ribaupierre, S., & Dubrowski, A. (2015). Measuring cognitive load during simulation-based psychomotor skills training: Sensitivity of secondary-task performance and subjective ratings. *Advances in Health Sciences Education: Theory and Practice, 20*(5), 1237–1253. https://doi.org/10.1007/s10459-015-9599-8

Henshall, C., Marzano, L., Smith, K., Attenburrow, M.-J., Puntis, S., Zlodre, J., Kelly, K., Broome, M. R., Shaw, S., Barrera, A., Molodynski, A., Reid, A., Geddes, J. R., & Cipriani, A. (2017). A web-based clinical decision tool to support treatment decision-making in psychiatry: A pilot focus group study with clinicians, patients and carers. *BMC Psychiatry, 17*(1), 265. https://doi.org/10.1186/s12888-017-1406-z

Hew, K., Bai, S., Dawson, P., & Lo, C.K. (2021). Meta-analyses of flipped classroom studies: A review of methodology. *Educational Research Review, 33*, 100393. https://doi.org/10.1016/j.edurev.2021.100393

Jia, C., Hew, K., Bai, S., & Huang, W. (2021). Adaptation of a conventional flipped course to an online flipped format during the Covid-19 pandemic: Student learning performance and engagement. *Journal of Research on Technology in Education*, 1–21. https://doi.org/10.1080/15391523.2020.1847220

Moffitt, R. L., Padgett, C., & Grieve, R. (2020). Accessibility and emotionality of online assessment feedback: Using emoticons to enhance student perceptions of marker competence and warmth. *Computers & Education, 143*, 103654. https://doi.org/10.1016/j.compedu.2019.103654

Mohan, D., Farris, C., Fischhoff, B., Rosengart, M. R., Angus, D. C., Yealy, D. M., Wallace, D. J., & Barnato, A. E. (2017). Efficacy of educational video game versus traditional educational apps at improving physician decision making in trauma triage: Randomized controlled trial. *British Medical Journal (Clinical Research Edition), 359*, j5416.

Perry, B., Stanton, C., & Janzen, K. (2022). *Pedagogy of kindness*. Generis Publishing.

Rawle, F. (2021, August 20). A pedagogy of kindness: The cornerstone for student learning and wellness. *Times Higher Education*. https://www.timeshighereducation.com/campus/pedagogy-kindness-cornerstone-student-learning-and-wellness

Stephens, L. E. (2021). More than students… a pedagogy of kindness. *SCHOLE: A Journal of Leisure Studies and Recreation Education, 38*(2), 1–2. https://doi.org/10.1080/1937156X.2021.1986434

Torrens Global Education. (2021). *Learning and teaching philosophy and principles*. Torrens University Australia (TUA).

Wanner, T., & Palmer, E. (2015). Personalising learning: Exploring student and teacher perceptions about flexible learning and assessment in a flipped university course. *Computers & Education, 88*, 354–369. https://doi.org/10.1016/j.compedu.2015.07.008

Chapter 5

The muscular realities of enacting a PoK in teaching practice

Charlotte Overgaard, Jacqueline Mackaway, Debra Adelaide, Lauren E. Stephens and Matthew Harrison

Introduction

The act of teaching is at once a deeply intimate and highly professional relationship. Teaching, when it's done well, is about transformation, those most magical of moments when a learner's awareness suddenly shifts. Something wakes up. Teachers know this and it is rewarding and wonderful when it happens. Many people tell a story of how a teacher saw them, inspired them, showed them something about themselves, gave them a pathway of possibility and knowledge that took them into another world of being and knowing and seeing. Yet transformation isn't always easy for the learner – or for the teacher.

In this chapter, five educators share stories about some of the practical realities of enacting a PoK in their teaching. Charlotte Overgaard and Jacqueline Mackaway note that having a 'sentiment of kindness' is not enough and describe ways they've enacted that sensibility in their daily practice. Debra Adelaide writes about maintaining kindness in the long-term supervisor relationship, while Lauren Stephens describes the gritty realities of teaching, encouraging mutual respect, and the importance of relationship building. Matthew Harrison writes about valuable lessons learned from working with an autistic pre-service teacher.

Turning kindness into practice

Charlotte Overgaard and Jacqueline Mackaway

Let us introduce some complaints about students we're sure you've heard in your daily work. If you do not know these arguments in your work, you have most certainly heard them in the media. These complaints sound like: 'students are not motivated', 'students lack capabilities', 'they don't even bother to show up', 'they are lazy'. The worst students, according to these criticisms, are those who are judged to be lacking in capabilities and are lazy. These students would be better off somewhere else – for their own good – it is argued.

Against such notions and dire views of students, a pedagogy of kindness (PoK) has become our anchor. This anchor is made up partly of a sentiment

DOI: 10.4324/9781003364887-5

that helps us imagine our students in other ways than described above and partly as a set of teaching practices which follow from that sentiment. As former colleagues in the Discipline of Sociology at Macquarie University, we consciously set out on a journey, an exploration of PoK and its potential and limitations. Here, we wish to expose what kindness means as a sentiment and as a teaching practice, a way to design for care – and bring PoK to the fore of teaching practices.

PoK, a sentiment and a practice

First, a word about kindness as a sentiment. While a sentiment is not enough, it is a necessary place to start. To enact any kindness, we must reimagine students differently to the notions described earlier. That is, if you wish to enact kindness, a necessary first step is to assume that students are capable and that it is your job, your responsibility, to ensure students' retention, progression and, ultimately, success in their studies. Whining about students can be an outlet, but ultimately, it does not make students more likely to succeed.

In turning our sentiment into action, we follow Cate Denial (2019), who argues that kindness as a pedagogical practice 'distils down to two simple things: believing people, and believing in people'. This entails putting students at the centre of their own learning experience (Clegg & Rowland, 2010). But what does that mean in practical terms?

PoK in our own practice

In our teaching, we have employed, trialled and rolled out several kind practices. We share some of these here to use, adapt or reject, depending on context.

For example, we know that many students fear speaking in public. Our students are now given a choice in how they deliver presentations. They can choose between face-to-face in class, online via Zoom or a pre-recorded version. We see this as kind to not only those students with anxieties about public speaking but also those students with tight time schedules or difficulties planning their time (e.g., if they have caring responsibilities or precarious work situations). By offering options in ways that suit students' lived realities, we are not pretending to know which option is the better one for them.

Another kind measure is the use of flexible deadlines. One version of such flexibility (used with undergraduate students) allows students to submit a first draft of a task within the first 20 hours of working on a semester-long project involving external partners. Another version (used for postgraduate students) allows students to nominate their own preferred submission dates within the hard boundaries of the semester calendar without penalties for not submitting. An evaluation of this trial showed fewer dropouts compared to the previous semester. Perhaps most surprising to some, only one student missed the hard deadline of the marking period at the end of the semester and then only by one day. The trial also meant fewer administrative burdens for students and staff concerning applications for extensions.

Traditionally, we set learning objectives based on the premise that teaching staff know best about what students should learn. Trusting in students to know what they wish to gain from their degrees, we instead invited final-year students to help identify key criteria for marking rubrics. Anecdotally students, at minimum, appreciate having some control over their learning and by us inviting them to be involved signals to them that we believe in and trust them. Our own experience with this practice is that students have good insights into what they want to learn and are realistic about what sort of capabilities different subjects entail. Importantly, our 'kindness doesn't dissolve the demands of knowledge' (Clegg & Rowland, 2010, p. 724) or learning. Involving students in the co-design of marking criteria could easily be done with first- and second-year students in a scaffolded way, leading to more comprehensive involvement in self-directed learning in the final year of study.

The benefits and the challenges

While we focus on students when we say that kindness makes a difference, a sentiment supported by research (Clegg & Rowland, 2010; Overgaard & Mackaway, 2021), we want to make it clear that kindness ultimately benefits staff too. PoK has allowed us to reimagine our students as whole people in charge of their own lives, students who are capable but happen to have other 'stuff' in their lives, such as dependents, mental illness, jobs, housing and home problems. This has turned us into allies of students and forced us to teach the students we have, not the students we wished we had. We build our work on an ambitious vision of fairness as we have written about elsewhere (Overgaard & Mackaway, 2022), a vision in which teaching aims to create fair outcomes – in opposition to fairness in the process.

When we give talks about PoK, we have come to expect certain questions, so let us address some common ones. The first has to do with leniency regarding deadlines and concerns that we fail to prepare students for the workforce. In our view, students need a range of skills and capacities. Kindness and respect for others are as important as meeting deadlines.

Similarly, critics are concerned that teachers will be met with infinite numbers of demands, which makes their jobs more difficult. This is a valid concern. However, our own experiences tell us that there is as much time gained as spent. For example, having students set their own marking criteria is a job that does not need to be completed by staff. Similarly, when there are no hard deadlines, the administrative burden becomes less, not more.

A concern could be that teachers have to judge which needs are worthy of flexibility, and which are simply the result of low discipline and poor time management. In line with POK, this is not a judgement to be made by teaching staff. If the student finds they need more time, trust their judgement rather than try to guess their motivation.

However, one legitimate concern deserves to be mentioned. Institutional structures and discourses can make it difficult for teachers to be kind (Mariskind, 2014). It might be difficult to act out a kindness pedagogy when staff are not sufficiently supported by their institution (Walker et al., 2006). Ideally, we wish to see comprehensive responses at all levels to start creating better conditions for a pedagogy of kindness. Yet, even within the hostile institutional boundaries of Macquarie University, the changes outlined earlier were possible to make, and we contend that it is always possible to make some changes in the direction of PoK.

Respecting pain: Kindness amid failure

Debra Adelaide

I always thought I would be kind. The brutal editing on my first book publication had been so confronting that later, as a professional teacher of writing, I determined to hold to the memory of this experience. I will always acknowledge how difficult that was, I would remind myself. How much it hurt, having my precious words torn apart. I would never forget how even the kindest criticism can shatter an author's confidence.

Despite this, I still upset many students. It seemed to be part of the job description. Numerous times students told me, after the creative writing workshop or a supervisory meeting, how upset, angry, confronted, or resistant they had been at the time. One student told the whole class that I didn't know what I was talking about (although later, after she scraped through, she gave me a gift and said she should have listened to me from the start). Another insisted that his scientific study of ants was creative and tried to take my novel writing class; when I said no, as he had not completed the prerequisite subject, he sent abusive group emails saying I was gaslighting him and that I was not a safe person to be teaching.

But this story is about another student – I shall call her Edie – who was studying for a doctorate in creative writing. Edie was already a published author but in a genre different to the one in which she was now writing. At first, Edie had trouble accepting my guidelines on how her supervision would proceed. The former supervisor, who had left the university, had applied no rules, and Edie had spent the previous year doing whatever she liked. My rules included asking for draft material to be emailed a week before our scheduled meeting. Edie was not the only student to send material the night before, somehow expecting that a supervisor has nothing else to do, not even sleep, until a meeting. Nor was she the only one to email draft work and then several days later, after I would have written up feedback, tell me to forget about it, because she'd revised it or trashed it altogether. (There should be a word for this because it happens so often, a lecturer looking at the 10 or 15 pages they have carefully marked up, then discovering it's destined for the bin – perhaps the Germans have a word for it: they're good at complex situations.)

Another rule was to submit a draft chapter for feedback every month. None of Edie's previously published books had received ongoing feedback (which she regarded as interventionist), and she insisted she would never have any problems ultimately producing the words. But it wasn't the number of words that concerned me but, rather, the quality of them. It was essential for her to receive and reflect on feedback before progressing to the next chapter. Furthermore, the doctorate is not a book: later it may become a book, and many doctoral students do eventually have their creative projects published, but this is not to say the text can simply be lifted from the completed project and sent to a publisher.

The other problem, one of genre, fed directly into this. Edie's comfortable success as an author and her loyal readership had created an inflated sense of her expertise. But she was now writing something different and far more ambitious. I hinted that her old rules may not apply here. This problem was one we circled around in meeting after meeting. I would not say it bluntly, but she needed to question her skills and approaches to the craft of writing and reconsider her strengths and weaknesses.

The ambition of Edie's story was admirable but also problematic: she was aiming for a 150,000-word novel, far in excess of the word limit set by the university, and even selecting the most indulgent of examiners, I could not see this getting approval. Towards the end of our first year, I felt we were making limited progress. Edie's output was clearly not a concern, but she maintained that, as a well-published author with more novels published than me, she did not need most of my advice. Not even advice about her overuse of exclamation marks. Many arguments occurred because I would suggest changes and she would defend her original prose. I used pencil to annotate her draft work, but even that could not soften the blow to her of having long slabs of useless dialogue tightened or abundant adjectives excised.

I feared that my frustrations on several levels were spilling over into our meetings, but I liked and respected Edie and I did not want to sour the supervisory relationship. Equally, however, I wanted to help her write the best possible novel for her doctoral project. I didn't want it to be good enough – I wanted it to be better than anything else she had ever written. Isn't that the point of all our endeavours, creative or otherwise? Surely she wanted to improve as a writer, not stay stuck in the same groove?

Finally, in our last session for the year, I had to spell out what to me was obvious: Edie had elected to enrol in a doctorate, so did she not accept that she was here to learn? She took this very well, but when we moved onto the problems she was having in realising her main female character, to my dismay, I saw tears forming. I stopped our discussion and said I was sorry, that I didn't want to upset her and that we could end the meeting. However, she gamely elected to push on, and as we kept talking about this character, she tearfully expressed her fears about being unequal to the task of this project.

By this time, I had also tried to understand why Edie always brought her young daughter and her nanny to our meetings. They would mostly play in the corridor outside my room, but I wondered why the nanny didn't mind the child at home. Now I realised that this was part of the performance, for my benefit as well as hers. The child – charming, intelligent, demanding – needed to be shown off to shore up Edie's ego. It was not deliberate; Edie had once mentioned several miscarriages, her final successful pregnancy in her mid-40s, her lack of family support. Then on this day of the tears, she explained how she had been over-encouraged to enrol in the doctorate. Finally, she broke right down, saying, 'I'm not good enough. I'll never do it.'

My heart wrenched. By this stage, I had shut the door on child, nanny and anyone else and was sitting close to her. It hit me that contrary to all appearances, Edie was completely lacking in confidence when it came to her doctoral project. Her parading of the appealing child was like her clinging to the prose style that had produced books that fed rather than challenged her readers' expectations. It was secure, known territory, even comforting. The 'readership' is a daunting, abstract concept, if not a commercial distraction, and often a hindrance to quality. I realised that to help Edie I had to put aside the writing for the moment and focus on the vulnerable human sitting next to me weeping.

I advised her to forget about her readers and choose one important person in her life and write for them. This was my approach, one that had always sustained me when the writing became too hard and failure loomed. Edie chose her husband. I suggested she try writing the next chapter with only him in mind.

I also reminded her of the stark reality of the doctoral readership: apart from me, three people would be reading this vast work. Very different to her thousands of existing fans. What if we were to discuss a list of those three possible examiners, people whom she respected and who might even inspire her? The identity of doctoral examiners is normally not revealed to students, but one can canvass a range of options before submission.

All this was a form of kindness, and it helped. The next draft chapter displayed a maturity and confidence that felt fresh and somehow more honest. Soon Edie was not bringing her child and her nanny to meetings. By the end of her candidature, she had independently solved the problem of the excessive length of her draft thesis. And when the examiners' reports finally returned, they were glowing. Edie's feedback for my supervision mentioned how grateful she was to have learned and grown as a writer.

And, of course, her book was eventually published. It even won a major award.

One lesson to be learnt from this is that individual context is all: my wealth of supervisory expertise on experimental processes, targeted deadlines, structural approaches, and so on, was less valuable than that light personal touch.

Another lesson is about the full meaning of student-centred learning, which is that its natural inverse is teacher-centred teaching: by this, I don't mean making the teaching about us but rather harnessing what challenged us into better learners to help address the weaknesses of our students. And a final lesson concerns understanding how pain and failure are necessary to improve thinking and knowledge, indeed, as US author and educator bell hooks (1994) explained, to 'respect that pain'. Just as we did, our students have considerable inner resources to get them through.

Inviting kindness into my classroom

Lauren E. Stephens

I was six months into my rookie year as a faculty member when the COVID-19 pandemic broke out in March 2020. Although not new to teaching thanks to a background in secondary education, I was new to the role of lecturer in the Department of Parks, Recreation and Tourism Management at Clemson University, an R1 university in the southeastern United States. As a department, we are known for being people-focused and student-centered, two principles that I knew, in theory, formed the essence of my teaching but, in practice, had just taken what I perceived to be a major hit with the onset of a pandemic with social distancing as a primary mitigation strategy.

It was during this time, in March 2020 as I was rethinking elements of my teaching philosophy and practices to meet the needs of my students, that I was introduced to the pedagogy of kindness through independent reading and discussion with trusted colleagues who shared Cate Denial's article "A Pedagogy of Kindness" with me. And, quite frankly, that changed everything.

What struck me most about Cate's article was her statement that "[k]indness is something most of us aspire toward as people, but not something we necessarily think of as central to teaching" (Denial, 2019, para. 6). And the question I just didn't have a good answer to was, "Why not?"

Inviting kindness into your classroom doesn't come without its own concerns – concerns around truth and accountability, for example – and I will be the first to acknowledge that. However, in light of the mental health crisis our colleges and universities are facing around the globe (What to Become, 2022), I echo Denial's position that I would rather take the risk of being lied to than make life more difficult for my students struggling with grief and illness, or even an overpacked schedule or computer trouble. It costs me nothing to be kind.

Because as I understand it, the pedagogical practice of kindness is not about sacrificing myself, or even about "being nice." Honest conversations, I would argue, are often not "nice." But they are necessary. And it is through these honest conversations – an act of kindness in themselves – that I grow and that my students grow.

Relationship building

When I think about the practical application of a pedagogy of kindness, it is grounded in the idea of treating students as people first and students second (Stephens, 2023), and for me, this manifests primarily as two distinct, yet related, concepts: (1) seeing and knowing my students as people, which leads to the development of mutual trust and respect, and (2) empowering my students through ownership in the course and giving them the space to ask for what they need.

I cannot undersell the importance of building trust in the classroom because it is when we feel safe enough to trust others that we are willing to be seen and known by them. I believe one of the best strategies for fostering trust is through showing my students that I care about them on a personal level (Bernstein, 2019). Through simple, yet intentional, acts of humanizing my students, such as learning what makes them unique or being interested in what is going on in their lives outside of our class, my students learn not only to trust me but also to trust each other.

Typically, this relationship building, although it sounds obvious, takes place at the start of class – and from the very first day of class – and I make a concerted effort not just to learn student names and interests but to really learn who my students are as well. For in-person classes, I set aside time at the beginning of the first day of class (or the first few days of class if I am teaching a bigger section) to ask students to share their names and a fun fact that I can remember them by, and we don't move into content until I have these nailed down. In the following few class periods, I'll take a couple of minutes to review these names and facts, a practice that both helps me see my students as unique humans and demonstrates to them that I am personally invested in each of them. For online classes, I'll log into the virtual space a few minutes early and pose a question such as "What's on your mind tonight?" or "What are you looking forward to this week?" for the students to respond to. It is through questions like these that a foundation of mutual trust, care, and respect is formed – not only between me and the students but between the students as well.

Empowering students

Empowering students and giving them the space to ask for what they need is another core element of the pedagogy of kindness, grounded in this understanding that our students are humans and that, as such, they are complex people with complex needs. Although I have been aware of this sentiment broadly for years, I was reminded again of the importance of this reality this past semester, as one of my students was balancing a full class schedule and a six-month-old at home. On two occasions, the student was courageous enough to ask for an extension on an assignment so that they could negotiate the requirements of being both parent and student – an extension I was thrilled to grant. I think there are two takeaways here: first, that the student felt comfortable advocating for their needs, which I credit to the pedagogy of kindness on which our course was structured, and, second, that they asked when they needed the extension and not just when they wanted it. Mutual trust and respect.

Empowering students also includes giving them both a voice and a platform for ownership, and I endeavor to do this weekly through another questioning strategy – this time, asking students for feedback about how we can improve the course design or class sessions in a way that supports their learning.

Adapting to change

This weekly check-in process with students is what led to the biggest change in course design during the Spring 2020 semester when I was first getting my feet wet with the pedagogy of kindness. In a typical semester, this particular class required students to submit an interview and application paper, as well as a final written essay exam, all within about a week of each other at the end of the term. However, as we approached the middle of April, which was about a month into quarantine, it became evident to me that the purpose I had for including both written assignments in the course was not being recognized by my students, who were struggling to keep their head afloat not only in their classes but also in life generally. Between not being able to return to their dorms to collect their belongings; trying to adjust to a fully online class schedule, especially when most of their courses had been designed for in-person face-to-face instruction; and managing the stress and uncertainty of a pandemic they didn't see coming, I came to the realization that the mountains of assignments my students were up against in all their courses were no longer facilitating learning but were in many ways hindering it.

And so, we modified our course. Instead of completing both written assignments, my students had the option of which assignment to prepare for and submit; this choice in which assignment to complete conveyed to the students that they were not passive participants in this situation, with things being done to them, but rather that I expected them to remain active contributors to their learning, doing things for themselves, despite the hand they'd been dealt. I did make slight changes to both assignments to ensure overlap of learning objectives so that having students complete either singular assignment would not compromise student learning outcomes. For me, the importance of this modification was not about "being nice"; it was a demonstration of kindness and the understanding that something much larger than an additional assignment was at stake.

Kindness is care

Although I cannot honestly say that making large course-level modifications is always easy – certainly, there are institutional expectations and traditional conventions to consider – I am confident that it is worth it. One of the greatest parts of being human is being known, and the pedagogy of kindness celebrates this fact by acknowledging that compassion and rigor are not antithetical. The pedagogy of kindness is not asking us to care about our students or to care about their learning. It's asking us to care, plain and simple.

A call for kindness and understanding for autistic students in initial teacher education

Matthew Harrison

In 2019, I participated in a mentoring program for early-career academics. Early in the program, all 40 program participants lined up from those who had been at the university for the least amount of time, to those who had served the longest. Even though I had been a teacher trainer for a number of years by this stage, I was surprised to learn from my position in this line that I was relatively early in my career. I discussed this revelation with my partner later that day. Whilst I saw it as a weakness in that I still had a lot to learn, she reframed it as a rare opportunity to change entrenched practices at an intuition that carried significant cultural weight. She helped me see the possibilities of making incremental but significant changes in how we prepare the next generation of teachers to better support different kinds of learners and learning. At the centre of these changes was rethinking the norms of my institution to enact a pedagogy of kindness in how we supported neurodivergent teacher candidates.

'Neurodiversity' was conceptualised by an Australian researcher, Judy Singer. In her seminal thesis, Singer (1999) reflected on her personal experiences of navigating a world constructed with a narrow set of norms and expectations that aligned with the needs of the neurotypical majority. At the centre of Singer's transformative thesis was a reconceptualisation of conditions such as autism and attention-deficit hyperactivity disorder presenting as differences rather than deficits (Chapman, 2020). Autism in particular has come to be seen as a unique culture, with an increasingly energised advocacy community looking to reframe the traditional understanding based on medical and psychological frameworks. Education has often been ahead of the game in promoting social justice (Naylor et al., 2022), leading other fields such as speech pathology in embracing these calls from our neurodivergent communities for this reframing.

A pedagogy of kindness is contextually bound, manifesting in different forms in different contexts. As Denial (2019) argues, applying such a philosophy in higher education is more about positionality and pedagogical patience than simply 'being nice'. In the context of training neurodivergent teachers, applying a pedagogy of kindness means listening to our teacher candidates to help us understand their cultural lens and asking how we can remove the barriers they experience in accessing our neurotypically normed schools.

In this chapter, I share (with their permission) the case of Samus (pseudonym), an autistic teacher candidate with whom I worked early in my career. Unfortunately, at that stage of my career, my understanding of her needs was not at a level where I could be effective in advocating for her. However, through my failure in helping Samus, I learnt some valuable lessons about the systematic tensions that can prevent us from implementing a pedagogy of kindness in teacher preparation programs. Following the experiences shared in this chapter, Samus provided a series of recommendations that I hope will help you better support the neurodivergent students in your tertiary education programs.

Meeting Samus

My first teaching opportunity at the Hyrule School of Education (pseudonym) occurred whilst completing my doctoral studies, tutoring in the technologies in primary education subject. At this time, I was also the digital technologies coordinator at a special development school for two days a week. I felt comfortable with the content that I would be covering as I had a wealth of experience that I could draw on to provide practical examples for my students. While working with adults definitely had some unique variables, I found the principles of effective teaching and learning to be surprisingly similar to working with children and young adults. The adult students I worked with on Wednesdays shared some of the intrinsically human needs with the seven-year-old students I taught on Thursdays and Fridays. It was when I was facilitating this class that I first met Samus, an enthusiastic teacher candidate. Following a class in which I mentioned my doctoral research and my teaching experience largely being focused on supporting autistic students, she waited behind as her peers left the room. Once we were alone, Samus confided in me that she was autistic. Having people who are close to me who are autistic, I had suspected this from some of her differences in social communication and interaction. I thanked her for feeling safe enough to share this with me and asked her if she wanted to get a coffee somewhere away from the teaching spaces so she could freely speak.

We got our coffees and headed to a quiet space, and then she told me about the battles her family faced in getting her access to a mainstream primary school, her social challenges at high school, and finally her present situation in completing her first placement as a pre-service teacher within a school. Academically, at the university, Samus was flourishing, but the initial observation day that preceded her placement period had not gone well. She reported that she found the children to be wonderfully accepting of her and her social differences, but she found the staff to be hostile from the outset. Samus found unexpected social situations difficult, so she had been working with a psychologist to practise her 'small talk' with adults. Despite her best attempts, the teachers at this first school had told her that she needed to act 'more natural' for the children and that she needed to essentially model neurotypical behaviours such as 'appropriate' eye contact. Ignoring the fact that norms around eye contact are highly subjective depending on culture, the staff had apparently judged Samus based on her appearance and decided that these children would be in some hypothetical danger if she was allowed in their classroom. There may have been other grounds for their discomfort, but in my interactions with Samus, I never once saw any indication she presented any risk to anyone. She was quiet, thoughtful, and if anything, overly empathetic for her peers and those in her charge.

Samus continued her placement until she received a phone call from the university's placement team that she was no longer welcome at the school. Despite the best efforts of Samus and the university support staff, the supervising teachers did not believe she had made sufficient progress as a teacher candidate. There undoubtedly would have been other reasons why this placement was cancelled beyond the manifestations of her neurological differences, but I have a distinct memory of feeling uncomfortable when she told me this news. Much of the feedback Samus shared with me was related to how she presented herself and how she communicated with others. At the time, it occurred to me that something was wrong with the system when a person with a passion such as Samus's and a clear disability could not access the environmental supports required to complete her first placement. As she was not publicly 'out' as an autistic person, the university had no grounds under the disability legislation to challenge the decision of the school. Samus later dropped out of the course and went on to complete her degree at another university.

Samus's recommendations to remove barriers for other neurodivergent students

Years later, we caught up for coffee. In the time between her failed placement and her completion of a teaching degree elsewhere, I had shifted from teaching ICT to coordinating autism intervention in the Master of Learning Intervention programme. I often make the observation that the focus of the majority of interventions to support autistic students is not with the child but within the culture and mindsets of the school community. Samus indicated that she wanted to debrief about her experiences at the Melbourne Graduate School of Education (MGSE). She shared her thoughts, and I tried my best to be empathic as someone who will never experience the challenges she faced during her first placement and will likely continue to face throughout her career. I asked her, upon reflection, what she would have wanted the university to do differently to better support her. She shared three responses that I have carried with me since this conversation. Although these recommendations related specifically to the manifestations of her autism, I believe they would more broadly support all university students.

Recommendation 1: Creating a culture of safety for autistic students to talk about their needs

Samus's first suggestion related to her feeling a lack of support at the school. She had lacked the confidence to speak to either her supervising teacher or the school principal about being autistic. Having someone she could trust and turn to would have helped. It is important to note that at the time, she was wary of telling anyone in a position of authority that she was autistic. This was especially true when she considered telling the school staff, as she felt this would make her even more of an outsider. She now wishes that they had been told she was autistic from the very start of her placement. She was fairly confident that having fellow student teachers working in the same environment who were aware of her diagnosis could have provided her, at the very least, with a sounding board. Of course, these other student teachers would have had to have been willing and felt safe enough given their own dependent positions to speak up for Samus. To address this power imbalance, Samus would have liked for the Student Equity and Disability Support staff from the university to have been actively involved with the school from the outset to educate her supervising teacher about some of the specific differences and challenges that those in the autistic community can experience in schools. Unfortunately, due to her wariness, she hadn't told anyone other than me at the university. When discussing this with her in later years, her message around communicating needs seemed to be about creating an atmosphere where pre-service teachers felt safe to talk about issues or challenges they might be facing.

From these conversations, I have learnt the importance of cultural safety. Creating dedicated cultural spaces for autistic students to express their needs and concerns is vital within the university environment. We start to build trust through the ways we discuss disability and neurological differences in our classes, our tutorials and informal discussions with individual students. When trust begins to be established, spaces emerge that enable autistic individuals to share their unique perspectives and requirements with university staff and their placement schools. The university plays a pivotal role in facilitating this process and should be actively collaborating with partner schools to ensure that placements are inclusive and accommodating for all students. Educating placement schools about autism and challenging prevailing stereotypes is essential in fostering an inclusive atmosphere. By dispelling misconceptions and promoting understanding, universities can help eliminate barriers that hinder the integration of autistic individuals into educational settings. This education can encompass raising awareness about the sensory sensitivities, communication differences, and diverse learning styles that may be associated with autism. I like to think of creating space as a form of pre-emptive institutional kindness, assuming that every year there will be some students who are autistic and who have a lifetime of experiences that make them wary about telling others of their specific challenges and needs.

*Recommendation 2: Share case studies of neurodivergent
pre-service teachers*

Samus would have liked to have had the opportunity to access case studies of other autistic students who had successfully completed teaching placements. If she could have read about their experiences, including their strategies for navigating the differences in social communication and interactions with staff, it may have better prepared her for what was to come. Being able to review and consider the lived experiences of others in a similar position to herself may have provided concrete guidance on managing the unspoken social rules that exist within schools. There were codes she was uncertain about, for example, how and when should you speak to other staff in the staff room? When is it okay to contact your supervising teacher? and How often should you request feedback from your supervising teacher? Of course, there would be differences from school to school, but providing case studies would share some of the experiences of peers.

As more autistic teacher candidates feel comfortable sharing their experiences of navigating school placements, these stories could be collated and shared as a means of building the confidence of future autistic candidates. The practical strategies and insights from these stories could be used by teacher educators to help autistic pre-service teachers navigate potential obstacles; address crucial aspects such as disclosure of autism, self-advocacy, and establishing effective communication channels; and offer examples of how to handle difficult conversations, address misunderstandings, and foster positive relationships with colleagues, students, and parents. Furthermore, these case studies could be used to help break down stereotypes and misconceptions surrounding autistic individuals as teachers. They could highlight the strengths, talents, and unique perspectives that autistic teachers bring to the classroom, promoting a more inclusive and diverse teaching workforce.

Recommendation 3: Establish a support network

Samus's third suggestion built on this idea of sharing a series of cases. Samus believed that a university-wide network for grassroots advocacy by those with experience of autism or neurodivergence is long overdue. Stanford University provides one such model, with its cross-facility Neurodiversity Project providing education for the general population and supporting neurodivergent staff and students in all facets of university life. By having a vehicle to raise awareness of the day-to-day challenges experienced by students such as Samus, our faculty could have been better equipped to predict and pre-emptively support autistic pre-service teachers as they engaged in their practicums. This could have provided a timely feedback loop to the university that there might be a broader issue with how we are supporting our students as they engage in their teaching placements.

Establishing peer support networks that are autistic-led for autistic teacher candidates is another important layer of support, particularly during the crucial phase of completing their teaching rounds. While we aspire to support all our teacher candidates through a pedagogy of kindness, there are times when those of us without lived experience need to step back. Encouraging these networks is one way we can do this. Autistic-led peer support networks empower teacher candidates by fostering a sense of belonging and community. They provide a platform for sharing experiences, challenges, and strategies specific to autism, creating an environment of mutual understanding and empathy. This allows autistic teacher candidates to develop their professional skills while embracing their neurodiversity. By connecting with peers who have navigated similar experiences, teacher candidates can connect on both a professional and personal level. Mentorship is at the centre of these networks, with autistic teacher candidates offering each other advice, encouragement, and somewhere safe to go when things don't work out as hoped.

Actualising these recommendations to enact a pedagogy of kindness in teacher education

I believe that enacting a pedagogy of kindness asks that we place the lived experiences of our students at the very centre of what we do. As the world becomes increasingly aware of neurodiversity and all that entails, we need to find new ways of supporting higher education students who experience systemic barriers in many facets of their education. Samus's recommendations provide a concrete starting point for teacher educators to do just this. I believe that we need teachers from all backgrounds and with all life experiences in order to connect authentically with our diverse student population. If this is to include students such as Samus, we need to listen to those voices and work collaboratively to develop pathways to success for everyone. Importantly, a pedagogy of kindness does not equate with lowering expectations for neurodivergent individuals to complete professional placements, but rather, it is about reconsidering what really constitutes an effective teacher and ensuring that we give our pre-service teachers the best possible chance to learn and develop.

References

Bernstein, J. (2019, June 24). TEACHER VOICE: I started seeing a difficult student as a person, not a 'challenge,' and it changed my outlook on education. *The Hechinger Report*. https://hechingerreport.org/the-mentor-who-taught-me/
Chapman, R. (2020). Defining neurodiversity for research and practice. In H. Rosqvist, N. Chown, & A. Stenning (Eds.), *Neurodiversity studies* (pp. 218–220). Routledge.
Clegg, S., & Rowland, S. (2010). Kindness in pedagogical practice and academic life. *British Journal of Sociology of Education, 31*(6), 719–735. DOI: 10.1080/01425692.2010.515102

Denial, C. (2019, August 15). A pedagogy of kindness. *Hybrid Pedagogy.* https://hybridpedagogy.org/pedagogy-of-kindness/

hooks, bell (1994). *Teaching to transgress: Education as the practice of freedom.* New York.

Mariskind, C. (2014). Teachers' care in higher education: Contesting gendered constructions. *Gender and Education,* (26), 306–320.

Naylor, A., Harrison, M., & Spence, S. (2022). Cultural responsiveness and diversity. In K. Barker, S. Poed, & P. Whitefield (Eds.), *School-wide positive behaviour support* (pp. 128–146). Routledge.

Overgaard, C., & Mackaway, J. (2021). Kindness as a push-back and designing for care. *Macquarie University's Teaching Blog, Teche.* Available at: https://teche.mq.edu.au/2021/03/kindness-as-a-push-back-and-designing-for-care/

Overgaard, C., & Mackaway, J. (2022). Kindness as a practice of Kittay's 'doulia' in higher education: Caring for student carers during COVID-19 and beyond. *International Journal of Care and Caring, 6*(1–2), 229–245. Policy Press. DOI: 10.1332/239788221X16330155145617

Singer, J. (1999). 'Why can't you be normal for once in your life?' From a 'problem with no name' to the emergence of a new category of difference. In M. Corker & S. French (Eds.), *Disability discourse.* Open University Press.

Stephens, L. E. (2023). More than students… A pedagogy of kindness. *SCHOLE: A Journal of Leisure Studies and Recreation Education, 38*(2), 136–137. DOI: https://doi.org/10.1080/1937156X.2021.1986434

Walker, C., Gleaves, A., & Grey, J. (2006). A study of the difficulties of care and support in new university teachers' work. *Teachers and Teaching, 12,* 347–363.

What to Become. (2022). 31 alarming college student mental health statistics. *Whattobecome.com.* Retrieved from: https://whattobecome.com/blog/college-student-mental-health-statistics/

Chapter 6

Storying unlearning for intended, enacted and felt kindness in online environs

Implications and opportunities for people, pedagogies and place

Abbey MacDonald

"What's this then?" I hear you ask.
Why would anyone want to unlearn being kind?
You're forgiven in advance for thinking this might be my intended
meaning here, but a moment of confusion is precisely where I hope to
position you as you step into this chapter.

Being kind and becoming kind are quite different things
and
not knowing how to be or do either doesn't necessarily mean that you're mean.

What I *mean* by this is that intended kindness does not in and of itself necessitate felt kindness. What might feel kind and benevolent for the person acting in and with intended kindness might be perceived or felt otherwise. Just because I want and try to be good and kind in my actions doesn't guarantee I will come across or be felt this way.

Still confused?
That's good and fine.
So was/am I.

I think kindness is contingent on our ability to communicate it as such, and we must accept the vulnerable position of not being able to guarantee kindness. The potential of and for kindness exists in the doing that intersects personal and professional practices and processes. I liken this to a process-weighted approach to art making and teaching; the learning happens in the doing of the making, and the end product isn't always the best place to see where and if the intended (or some other unanticipated) learning – about kindness, for example – occurs.

We mustn't underestimate the role, influence, opportunities and limitations of the places where we attempt to 'be' kind. For those of us who find ourselves living aspects of our personal and professional lives in online spaces, the norms and parameters of what we individually and collectively define as 'kind' and

DOI: 10.4324/9781003364887-6

enact/embrace as 'kindness' are being reimagined. The tangible and intangible layers of interface that permeate our intra- and interpersonal communications feel much more complex and, these days, a vast terrain to traverse. With communicative limitations for non-verbals, body language and energy that aren't yet necessarily transcending the digital interface, kindness doesn't always land in the ways we hope or intend. Digital places can be quite unforgiving of human mistakes and earnest attempts to take (sometimes for very legitimate and sometimes legally consequential reasons). At times it feels like we are struggling to accommodate yet another layer of learning and challenge in our attempts to communicate, connect and belong.

The relationship between being and becoming kind, and the role unlearning can play for what I describe as intended, enacted, and felt kindness, is complex and curious. I also feel like our conceptions of intended, enacted, and felt kindness can be quite wicked in the sense that our efforts to foster kindness can run into pre-existing wicked problems. As a person drawn to discursive playfulness, I enjoy thinking about all this from the space between kindness and wickedness.

In my thinking about kindness in online environs, I oscillate between Rittel and Webber's (1973), Conklin's (2001), and Head and Alford's (2015) conceptualisations of wicked problems, which comprise an evolving set of interlocking issues, constraints and possibilities. Wicked problems are characterised by complex and uncertain attributes, usually created (or at least compounded further) by multiple competing interests. I feel like this provides a really interesting thinking apparatus for moving between notions of intended, enacted and felt kindness in online environs.

The trouble with kindness is that it hangs on threads of expectation and hope in relation to that which our gestures (of kindness) are anticipated and offered. In the same way that an artist has limited control over people accepting the intended meaning of their artwork, there is very little we can do to *ensure* kindness is conveyed, received and reciprocated. Kindness isn't something that can be necessitated, promised or made foolproof. This is particularly the case in online environments where our usual tools and means for interpersonal communication are mediated, filtered through and (re)presented via ever-evolving digital interfaces.

There is simply a lot of unknowing and uncertainty involved with practising kindness in the online environment. As such, my chapter is not a 'how to be seen, heard and felt as kind online' as much as it is a 'how can I become comfortable with not being able to ensure I am seen, heard and felt as kind online? This is my unlearning story.

Positionality and context

Before we get into the what and the how, I'll begin with a bit about myself. Positionality is important, and I hope you'll come to see and appreciate my sentiment on this, particularly for relationality and unlearning, as you make your way through my chapter. For me, positionality and context inextricably entwine with relationality and unlearning. Before I go into that, however, I'll attempt to locate myself and my work as an online metho-pedagogue in the context of micro (individual/local), mezzo (institutional/national) and macro (global) synergies and connections (Coleman et al., 2021). I offer an expanded positionality that isn't just about me; it is also about me in relation, keeping consistent with my championing of unlearning. This will help you get a sense of the assumptions and biases that permeate my story, and the things I'm interested in, as well as allowing you to see, how my approach locates in and leverages the blurred edges between these three layers.

Micro positionality

I'm a non-Indigenous Australian woman of extensive Scottish, Irish and English ancestry. I am first-generation Australian on my dad's side and eighth generation on my mother's side. I was born, raised and continue to live in the Australian island state of Tasmania with my young family. I've worked as a teacher educator, predominantly an arts teacher educator, for 13 years. Of those 13 years, I've taught online for a decade. Except for delivering pre-service and in-service teacher professional learning events in person, I have facilitated initial teacher education (ITE) exclusively online for the past three years. I have learnt a great many things in that time and still feel every bit as green and unnerved as the day I began, simply because the landscape in which I live and teach online is changing constantly. This is because I am learning and unlearning, always.

My invitation to contribute to this exciting book about pedagogies of kindness was shepherded, I presume, through/to my teacher educator self and how I go about my business in that space. As a teacher educator, artist and researcher, I work in ways that are highly sensitised to the co-constitutive nature of pedagogy and methodology and think of this coupling as metho-pedagogy (MacDonald et al., 2022; Gallagher et al., 2022). The metho-pedagogical storying that permeates this chapter is brought to fruition via my own active unlearning. It comprises pieces of my personal and professional self and is assembled through my onto-epistemological frame for teaching from who I am (Palmer, 2017) unapologetically and in my entirety. I live and work with chronic illness, fibromyalgia, a condition that causes a widespread and sometimes unpredictable experience of pain throughout my body for no good reason. A literal and figurative pain in my arse and many other parts of my body.

A particular limitation for me is experienced in my intended/enacted kindness when I'm in the active pain of a 'fibro-flareup', which is both distracting and depletes my energy and patience. I am (be)coming to embrace this condition as equal parts frustrating and a terrific mediator for unlearning unkind work habits and respecting my body's voice and its limitations. A more recent diagnosis of combined attention-deficit hyperactivity disorder has presented another learning/unlearning opportunity. I am no longer putting energy into trying to conceal or deny these parts of myself personally or professionally and instead unlearning and discovering how to live and work in ways that better utilise what I am (be)coming to reframe as strengths. It is with these things and more that I strive to live with personal and professional authenticity, with what has passed and what is yet to come through an ongoing commitment to practise unlearning (Cochran-Smith, 2003; McWilliam, 2008).

A person's ability and need to be kind to oneself and those around them is an important part of the equation underlying this chapter's proposition. What a wicked problem this is! Every day I wrestle with feelings of misalignment, discomfort, not belonging and being able to be authentic in 'the academy', and I am not alone in this (Sikes, 2006). Wrestling with the prioritisation of professional and personal identities that feel in conflict rather than comple-ment is not well understood or managed in academia, particularly for those of us who are transitioning from one profession to another (MacDonald et al., 2014; MacDonald, 2017). Uncertainty breeds frustration and insecurity, which can be inherently destabilising (Laudel & Glaser, 2008). But the reality is we live in increasingly uncertain times that ask and indeed require us to become comfortable with not knowing.

As a person living in and with tangible and ambiguous discomfort, there are many further reasons why I paradoxically find myself feeling grounded in uncertainty. Bringing these to life through the medium of a textually rendered story can be affirming and validating. It remind us that when all voices are being heard through storying, regardless of positionality, "we can nurture relationships, form authentic collaborations and energise actions to support humanness in all our encounters" (p. 9). My positionality practised and intended here is not one that intends to or invites you to make comparisons between me and you or other things. I offer my positionality as part of a broader relational constellation in which we all know and do things in and from perspectives, some of which we must accept that we can never really know.

Mezzo positionality

I live and work on the unceded lands of the Palawa and Pakana people of Lutruwita/Tasmania as a Senior Lecturer in Arts Education at the University of Tasmania. I am a part and beneficiary of a colonial system reckoning with its deeply troubling history of theft, violence and subjugation. I have a role to play in the problem and solution and so can be many conflicting things concurrently.

It is fair to say that I am both adept and uncertain in my online teaching; both of these can be true and concurrent. Part of navigating my uncertainty is mediated by putting myself out there. My pedagogical approaches for online

teacher education have been recognised as innovative at the highest level insti-
tutionally, as well as nationally through my being awarded the Teachers Mutual
Bank–ATEA (Australian Teacher Education Association) Teacher Educator of
the Year in 2019. That was a few years ago now, and I can tell you that while
such awards are lovely to receive, and affirming in the face of uncertainty, they
do not make you impervious to either doing or finding yourself on the receiving end of not-so-lovely things. I continue to unlearn as I go.

I already mentioned that I live and work in Tasmania, which is the small
island state (surrounded by smaller islands) off the far southeast tip of conti-
nental Australia, over the Bass Strait from the mainland state of Victoria.
Tasmania boasts one of the most vibrant creative communities in Australia
concurrent to some of the lowest levels of educational attainment (MacDonald
et al., 2020), and this was pre-COVID-19. Today, in what I refer to as
COVID-normal times, the extremes of privilege and poverty have intensified,
with accentuated disadvantage experienced by already vulnerable groups. In
keeping with its paradoxical qualities, ingenuity, adaptability and innovation
have flourished elsewhere on the island (Wise et al., 2022). In other words,
intended acts of kindness and problem-solving have the potential to address
one problem, while creating or exacerbating another. For example, recent arts,
culture and education collaborative interdisciplinary research I contributed to
in Tasmania (Wise et al., 2022) revealed that public health lockdown measures
implemented during the COVID-19 pandemic meant that digital innovation
became both a significant enabler and inhibitor of people connecting with
each other and to place. This was a problem because not all families have the
quantity or quality of digital hardware and software necessary to ensure equitable access to or opportunity to participate in online education (Brown et al.,
2020). This broader context of digital and socio-economic inequity apparent in the wider landscape of education provision also affects my delivery of
online ITE.

Tasmania remains a complex place, contending with complex socio-
economic and environmental challenges. While it is fair to say Tasmania is
complex, I'm proud to have been taught and to work at an institution striving
to position itself as being 'place-based and globally relevant' in its strategic
research and education priorities. I love the this- *and* that-ness that must be
accounted for in any genuine ecology of kindness. It is also fair to say that I
have a sense of empathy and appreciation for the geographic and institutional
places in which I work. It is also fair to say that I harbour frustrations about
what I perceive as a lack of intended, enacted and felt kindness in these places
and the complex relations and spaces between them.

Macro positionality

In looking at and from the positionality and context of intended, enacted and
felt kindness, the micro and mezzo aspects sharpen my focus for zooming out

into a bigger picture macro composition. It is in the bigger picture that I prosecute the intentionality of kindness and the directions in which it extends.

Locally and globally, we live in a time where our sense of kindness continues to be challenged and we reimagine it as a result. Teachers – particularly across the arts – continue to show tremendous ingenuity in their response to prioritised financial investment in the STEM education agenda globally (UNESCO, 2022; Commonwealth of Australia, 2023a). Furthermore, their ingenuity and cleverness are achieved in the midst of escalating global uncertainty caused by a changing climate (Cole & Somerville, 2017; Nairn, 2019) and the ongoing COVID-19 pandemic (Coleman et al., 2020), all of which contribute to and exacerbate perennial educational problems in Australia, such as the digital divide and educational inequality (Ng & Renshaw, 2020) that I allude to at the micro and mezzo levels. I'd wager most of us can point and speak to both tangible and perceived opportunities we have benefitted from and obstacles that vex us. My family line is not characterised by plentiful stories of educational attainment, at least not when viewed through the prism of what I feel are very limited parameters for how educational attainment and subsequently 'success' is understood, measured and quantified today (Wise et al., 2022; Hunter & MacDonald, 2017). My family is full of stories of ingenuity, resilience, grit and determination, and those are the things that carry me forward.

In zooming out, I wonder about the very personally situated question, How does one look after themselves in their work? And by this, I mean keep safe and well, and whose responsibility is that? A quick look between mainstream media (MSM) commentary and a Google Scholar search of articles reporting on 'burnout in university teaching staff' presents a grim picture of academics not being looked after as well as being bad at taking care of ourselves. The former (MSM commentary) of course shoulders responsibility upon the shoulders of individuals rather than scrutinising the actual elephant in the room, which is the blatantly exploitative, insecurity fostering and deeply unkind professional system that is higher education (Mockler & Redpath, 2022). The same can be said for classroom schoolteachers and principals. We need only look at the most recent *Strong Beginnings: Report of the Teacher Education Expert Panel* (Commonwealth of Australia, 2023b) and the various reports in the decade preceding it to see the parallels of blame being placed on academics and schoolteachers for substandard education outcomes (Mockler, 2020; Mockler, 2022). Our intended, enacted and felt kindness continues to be challenged by the performance metric imperatives of the neoliberal university (Mcleod et al., 2020) by which we all continue to be judged today. Collectively, the way these measures are used to both dictate and scrutinise how we foster and practise kindness in online settings erodes wellbeing and separates us from each other as relational beings (Mcleod et al., 2020).

And so, here we are in 2023, in a 'COVID-normal' world, with its myriad intermingling layers of complexity and wicked attributes. The world has changed, and all of us with it, albeit in different ways. Here I am, still teaching online. Perhaps you are too. While the peak COVID 'pivot' online of early 2020 in Australia didn't cause me the anxiety that it caused for many of my friends and colleagues who had never taught online, it totally challenged and changed the parameters of intended, enacted and felt kindness in the teacher-learner encounter.

So, how do I survive and occasionally thrive in the online space? Through the equal parts simple and complex act of investing in relationships and relationality through an ongoing commitment to unlearn.

Relationality and unlearning in metho-pedagogical inquiry

I'll start with relationality, simply because for me, this came/comes first. For me, this practice of relationality is rooted in my 2014 PhD investigation, in which I sought to explore the ways that artist and teaching practices interact. Coming into that PhD as an artist and beginning teacher, I wanted to articulate and better understand the implications this artist–teacher relationality has upon beginning teachers' transition into professional practice. In the decade since my PhD, I continue to expand my understandings of relationality beyond my narrow artist-teacher focus.

Through ongoing attendance to unlearning, I continue to unlearn, expand and reconfigure my horizons of and for understanding what it means to teach relationally, particularly in online space where I have taught ITE exclusively for the past three years. While I'd have liked to have shared with you the practice-based aspects and possibilities of my metho-pedagogic inquiry, have instead prioritised alighting the conceptual architecture on which I assemble and pursue my process. For me relationality and unlearning are integral for making sense and meaning if intended, enacted and felt kindness in online environs, be it online teaching, research collaboration or initiatives that blur the edges between these (i.e. metho-pedagogy). You'll remember I described this chapter as not a 'how to be seen, heard and felt as kind online' as much as it is a 'how can I become comfortable with not knowing how to be seen, heard and felt as kind online? There is simply a lot of unknowing and uncertainty involved with practising kindness in the online environment. Relationality and unlearning are the overarching thinking tools that help me metho-pedagogically survive and occasionally thrive in this space.

The most powerful knowledge holders of and for relationality pedagogy are found in the work of Indigenous scholars, and their conceptions of relationality for ways of knowing, being and doing. For example, Burgess et al. (2022) and Suchet-Pearson et al. (2013) offer generous renderings that attend to the vibrant more-than-human relationality that lives and is fostered between people, place and pedagogic possibility. This knowledge, both ancient and sophisticated, is the ground in which the meagre roots of Western research paradigms and the historical narratives that permeate my own education sought to claim it as its own. This extends to Western methodological framings of narrative and reflective practice that, at best, omit and, at worst, obscure what very much looks, sounds and reads like a colonisation of storied ways of knowing, being and doing.

Phillips et al. (2018) describe that "for Aboriginal peoples, Stories are embodied acts of intertextualised, transgenerational Law and life spoken across and through time and place" (p. 8). They go further to offer a non-definitive list of five principles for storying:

1 Storying nourishes thought, body and soul;
2 Storying claims voice in the silenced margins;
3 Storying is embodied relational meaning-making;
4 Storying intersects the past and present as living oral archives; and
5 Storying enacts collective ownership and authorship.

In my writing of this chapter, I have enmeshed these with Mcleod et al.'s (2020) five principles for a pedagogy of unlearning:

1 Anticipate the discomfit of disruption;
2 Make small acts towards contexts that matter;
3 Shift attention to unlearning encounters;
4 Attune to the potential of the new; and
5 Accept the ongoing mix of un/learning.

Distinct to learning, unlearning couples the acquisition of new practices, knowledge and orientations, with identity, unravelling and reimagining habits expectations and norms that are no longer useful (Cochran-Smith, 2003; McWilliam, 2008). The latter part of the unlearning equation is hard, as many of those habits are rooted in uncomfortable biases, assumptions and preconceptions that have deep – sometimes transgenerational deep – roots. They require hard work to reconcile and reconfigure in ways that are healing and helpful. It is in my commitment to unlearning that I grapple with what I perceive to be the complex dimensionality of kindness in online environs: *Kindness intended*, *Kindness enacted* and *Kindness felt*.

In this moment, I return once more to the question, 'How can I become comfortable with not knowing how to be seen, heard and felt as kind online?' While I know I have no control over your 'read' and 'takeaway' of my story, these are the things I hope sing through as my intentionality.

For me, kindness 'becomes', in the Deleuzean sense where it is contextual (in place), contingent (upon people) and contiguous (pedagogically). Because of these mobile inter-relating parts, kindness is also very 'slippery' – in the Deleuze and Guattari (1988) sense – due to being both highly affective and arising from productive acts, as distinct to being a product or outcome in and of itself. I think about kindness as an entangled process-oriented triad of intentions, enactments and feelings that can yield new possibilities for becoming differently (MacDonald et al., 2022) in teacher education practice and research.

You'll recall earlier I introduced the notion of kindness in online environs as being both complex and wicked. This is because I find it to be resistant to blunt instruments or simple attempts to make sense and meaning of the practice and process of it all. I'm not trying to be clever when I suggest complex methodological and pedagogical thinking apparatuses present the most useful navigational tools. I have arrived at a point where I have stopped giving time and energy to trying to find or make simple solutions to complex, wicked things. I am instead trying to respect and go with complexity. I do this through attending to my own learning and unlearning through the prism of metho-pedagogy to discover things differently. Instead of going '*work with this OR that theory/pedagogy/methodological tool*', I '*work with this AND that theory/pedagogy/methodological tool*'. I put my time and energy into rendering the what, why and how for this, which is precisely what I am attempting to do in this chapter. Doing this can be super complicated, but it is embracing the uncertainty, unknowing and uncomfortable that prime me to deal with complexity and stay light on my feet as I move between things. I hope to see more and different storyings of these kinds of things.

As an act of metho-pedagogic unlearning, I draw attention to the thinking tools that help me both respect and navigate the uncertainty that permeates intended, enacted and felt kindness in online environs. Working with principles of storying and unlearning helps us scrutinise and better understand how the relational dimensions of and between people, pedagogies and places shape our experience of intended, enacted and felt kindness. I am thinking and writing specifically about this as a teacher educator who at this time is exclusively teaching online. I have sought to highlight the importance of living and working in ways that encourage authenticity and that we attend to this in ways that help us stay open to relationality and unlearning (McLeod et al., 2020). It is my hope that in doing so, we can reframe our efforts to define, contain and solve problems to more expansive relational ways of thinking, knowing and doing that facilitate concurrent learning/unlearning. These are the things that accommodate parallels and deliver serendipitous insights that only uncertainty, ambiguity and instability can provide. My own unlearning story is located in the contiguous space *between binaries* such as good and bad, simple and complex, practical and theoretical, material and digital, personal and professional. Through the prism of people, pedagogies and place, working with principles for storying and unlearning present incredibly helpful parameters for navigating intended, enacted and felt kindness in online environs.

On the topic of kindness (intended, enacted, felt) for pedagogical and methodological endeavour, reflexive attunement is essential and unlearning is a terrific enabler of reflexive practice. My practice of unlearning helps me keep attuned and across a great many things. It helps me keep my eyes, ears, mind and heart open. I read, listen and create with matter through technologies of paint and text, both of which entwine tangible matter with digital tools and online worlds. Technology is deeply rooted in art, and the far edge of digital innovation (i.e. artificial intelligence) that many of us are wrestling with trails a long tail that originates in practice-based origins of arts, craft and design (Asia & Gordon, 2021; MacDonald & Crowley, 2023). Things are changing all the time in the ITE space, particularly with respect to digital technologies. It feels like there's a new fandangled thing for us to contend with every five minutes. Blink and you'll miss it. Feelings of overwhelm and burnout erode our patience, spirit and capacities for giving and receiving kindness. I look forward to revisiting this chapter in 10 years' time and – hopefully – having a good laugh about how things evolved.

References

© Commonwealth of Australia (2023a). *Revive: A place for every story, a story for every place – Australia's cultural policy for the next five years.* https://www.arts.gov.au/sites/default/files/documents/national-culturalpolicy-8february2023.pdf

© Commonwealth of Australia (2023b). *Strong beginnings: Report of the teacher education expert panel.* https://apo.org.au/sites/default/files/resource-files/2023-07/apo-nid323424.pdf

Asia, D., & Gordon, R. E. (2021). Cultural value and evolving technologies: Instances from music and visual art. *Social Philosophy and Policy, 38*(2), 210–231.

Brown, N., Te Riele, K., Shelley, B., & Woodroffe, J. (2020). Learning at home during COVID-19: Effects on vulnerable young Australians. *Peter Underwood Centre for Educational Attainment.* https://www.utas.edu.au/__data/assets/pdf_file/0010/1411012/Brown-et-al-2020.pdf

Burgess, C., Thorpe, K., Egan, S., & Harwood, V. (2022). Learning from country to conceptualise what an aboriginal curriculum narrative might look like in education. *Curriculum Perspectives, 42*(2), 157–169.

Cochran-Smith, M. (2003). Learning and unlearning: The education of teacher educators. *Teaching and Teacher Education, 19*(1), 5–28.

Cole, D. R., & Somerville, M. (2017). Thinking school curriculum through country with Deleuze and Whitehead: A process-based synthesis. In C. Haughton, G. Biesta, & D. Cole (Eds.), *Art, artists and pedagogy* (pp. 71–82). Routledge.

Coleman, K., Selkrig, M., & MacDonald, A. (2021). Visual Arts Education/s: Glocal threads to connect, entangle, sustain and nourish during a prolonged lockdown and time of uncertainty. *Arts education in and through a time of crisis: The 4th UNESCO-UNITWIN symposium,* Seoul, Korea, 24–26 May http://www.arteweek.kr/assets/download/2021international_art_education_week_programbook_Eng_Final.pdf

Conklin, J. (2001). *Wicked problems and social complexity.* Retrieved March 7, 2022 from http://qi.speedwaystaging.co.uk/wp-content/uploads/2015/08/cn-wickedproblems.pdf

Deleuze, G., & Guattari, F. (1988). *A thousand plateaus: Capitalism and schizophrenia.* Bloomsbury Publishing.

Gallagher, K., Cardwell, N., Denichaud, D., & Valve, L. (2022). The ecology of global, collaborative ethnography: Metho-pedagogical moves in research on climate change with youth in pandemic times. *Ethnography and Education, 17*(3), 239–274. https://doi.org/10.1080.17457823.202202025879

Head, B. W., & Alford, J. (2015). Wicked problems: Implications for public policy and management. *Administration & Society, 47*(6), 711–739.

Hunter, M. A., & MacDonald, A. (2017). Dark play: On an alternative politics of aspiration. In P. O'Connor & C. Gomez (Eds.), *Playing with possibilities* (pp. 16–33). Cambridge Scholars Publishing.

Laudel, G., & Glaser, J. (2008). From apprentice to colleague: The metamorphosis of early career researchers. *Higher Education*, 55, 387–406. https://doi.org/10.1007/s10734-007-9063-7

MacDonald, A. (2017). A diptych of dilemma: Becoming an artist and a teacher. *International Journal of Education through Art, 13*(2), 163–177.

MacDonald, A., Coleman, K., Healy, S. & Diener, M. (2022). How does pedagogical slipperiness enable speculation in/for teacher professional learning? In E. Baumgartner (Ed.), *A retrospective of teaching, technology, and teacher education during the COVID-19 pandemic*, (1, pp. 45–49). Association for the Advancement of Computing in Education. https://www.insea.org/wp-content/uploads/2022/05/IMAG_issue_13.pdf

MacDonald, A., & Crowley, S. (2023). Tangible technologies: Opportunities and implications for junior high school teachers to connect practice, curriculum and pedagogies. In R. E. Ferdig, R. Hartshorne, E. Baumgartner, R. Kaplan-Rakowski, & C. Mouza (Eds.), *What pre K–12 teachers should know about educational technology in 2023: A research-to-practice anthology*. Association for the Advancement of Computing in Education (AACE) https://www.learntechlib.org/p/222690/

MacDonald, A., Cruickshank, V., McCarthy, R., & Reilly, F. (2014). Defining professional self: Teacher educator perspectives of the pre-ECR journey. *Australian Journal of Teacher Education (Online), 39*(3), 1–16.

MacDonald, A., Wise, K., Tregloan, K., Fountain, W., Wallis, L., & Holmstrom, N. (2020). Designing STEAM education: Fostering relationality through design-led disruption. *International Journal of Art & Design Education, 39*(1), 227–241.

McLeod, K., Thakchoe, S., Hunter, M. A., Vincent, K., Baltra-Ulloa, A. J., & MacDonald, A. (2020). Principles for a pedagogy of unlearning. *Reflective Practice, 21*(2), 183–197. https://journals.sagepub.com/doi/pdf/10.1177/1470412919875404

McWilliam, E. (2008). Unlearning how to teach. *Innovations in Education and Teaching International, 45*(3), 263–269.

Mockler, N. (2020). Discourses of teacher quality in the Australian print media 2014–2017: A corpus-assisted analysis. *Discourse: Studies in the Cultural Politics of Education, 41*(6), 854–870.

Mockler, N. (2022). *Constructing teacher identities: How the print media define and represent teachers and their work.* Bloomsbury Publishing.

Mockler, N., & Redpath, E. (2022). Shoring up "teacher quality": Media discourses of teacher education in the United Kingdom, United States, and Australia. In I. Menter (Ed.), *The Palgrave handbook of teacher education research* (pp. 933–961). Palgrave Macmillan.

Nairn, K. (2019). Learning from young people engaged in climate activism: The potential of collectivizing despair and hope. *Young, 27*(5), 435–450.

Ng, C., & Renshaw, P. (2020). Transforming pedagogies in Australian schools amid the COVID-19 pandemic: An activity theoretic reflection. *Best Evidence of Chinese Education, 5*(2), 635–648.

Palmer, P. J. (2017). *The courage to teach: Exploring the inner landscape of a teacher's life.* John Wiley & Sons.

Phillips, L. G., Bunda, T., & Quintero, E. P. (2018). *Research through, with and as storying.* Taylor & Francis.

Rittel, H. W., & Webber, M. M. (1973). Dilemmas in a general theory of planning. *Policy Sciences, 4*(2), 155–169.

Sikes, P. (2006). Working in a "new" university: In the shadow of the research assessment exercise. *Studies in Higher Education, 31*(5), 555–568.

Suchet-Pearson, S., Wright, S., Lloyd, K., Burarrwanga, L., & Bawaka Country. (2013). Caring as country: Towards an ontology of co-becoming in natural resource management. *Asia Pacific Viewpoint, 54*(2), 185–197.

UNESCO. (2022). *Education: From disruption to recovery.* https://www.unesco.org/en/covid-19/education-disruption-recovery

Wise, K., MacDonald, A., Badham, M., Brown, N., & Rankin, S. (2022). Interdisciplinarity for social justice enterprise: Intersecting education, industry and community arts perspectives. *The Australian Educational Researcher, 49*(3), 595–615.

Chapter 7

Kindness, creativity, productive failure, and agency

An exploration with an example from educational research

Edwin Creely

Introduction

In this chapter, I engage with several key ideas about education and about learning that I consider to be vital not only for the future but also for sustaining what is valuable at the very heart of education: developing learners who are innovative, resilient, group-oriented and most of all, kind. One of the foremost concerns is moving beyond derogatory notions of failure that are often implicit and explicit in education towards seeing failure in learning as the key to building a range of competencies valuable in terms of navigating uncertain futures where there may well be challenges that all students face as they go into work and study beyond school (Henriksen et al., 2019). Opening the notion of failure as a strength in learning also potentially expands the horizons of students and is, I believe, a vital component of a pedagogy of kindness because it allows students to become agential and afforded the opportunity to be self-directed and lifelong learners. Kindness, for me, is ultimately about engendering freedom and allowing our students to find, through focused support, what brings them happiness, a sense of belonging and fulfilment.

To illustrate these ideas, I offer a research example from my own research experience as a teacher educator and academic at a University in Melbourne, Australia. The example is from a large research project involving Year 8 teachers at a secondary school (Creely et al., 2021). This example focuses on mathematics education, which can often be viewed as especially oriented to the textbook and well-honed systematic approaches in mathematics and numeracy education.

In this writing, my authorial voice is front and centre to bring the reader a sense of my own experiences, views, and outlook on education and the research that informs it. It is thus an autoethnographic and narrative approach that reveals my values and thinking as an educator and researcher with over 40 years of experience in the Australian context (Ellis et al., 2011). While these issues were identified as especially relevant to concerns in Australia, the research literature suggests that such concerns are also relevant internationally, including in the Asian region. Of course, I make no claims that my views are in any way

DOI: 10.4324/9781003364887-7

definitive, but I hope that they provoke thinking and open debate about the nature of the work that educators do and the larger picture about what education should be about and who it is for. At the forefront, as far as I am concerned, is the growth of students as lifelong independent creative and critical learners.

The educational context of my thinking about kindness

In all sectors of education, the emphasis in teaching and learning has typically been on the delivery of content, assessing competencies and achieving outcomes, especially when it comes to core literacy and numeracy skills that are pivotal to participation in society in education, work and civil engagement. In the last 30 years in Australia, where I live, and internationally, there has been a noticeable shift to high-stakes testing to provide an evidentiary basis for learning and standardised outcomes, but this has meant a narrowing of how students are assessed, especially on quantifiable tasks (Kohn, 2000; Au, 2011). Many educators and academics, including me, have questioned the narrow scope of such an emphasis in assessment practices and the contraction of what is deemed assessable and thus valued and what is not towards a culture of compliance. Indeed, there are assessment tasks that are more difficult to quantify but contain deeper learning in the form of higher order thinking that includes critical thinking, creativity and so-called soft skills, such as personal and social capabilities (Darling-Hammond & Adamson, 2010).

I believe learning in critical areas such as literacy and numeracy needs a more holistic approach and a broader scope of practices to do with learning and assessment. One of my core concerns is that teachers, if they work under the regime of a narrow way of assessing, will teach to the test, the prescribed curriculum, and the textbook and thus not bring enough emphasis to learning in its holistic sense of being lifelong, about agency and about full participation in society as an informed citizen capable of adaptation and critical thought (UNESCO, 2015). I believe this is especially important now given the rate of change and the digitisation of society, including the emergence of artificial intelligence in education. Moreover, education is more than about understanding, skills and competencies. It is also about values and how education can develop students with an ethical and critical outlook on the world, including, I might add, being kind to fellow human beings and the earth on which we all depend.

To this I would add as a core concern the need to incorporate risk-taking and productive failure in education (Creely et al., 2019). An orientation to certain specified assessment outcomes and teaching to the test tend to diminish the possibilities of students engaging in riskier, inquiry-based and experimental ways of learning. Through embracing the possibilities that emerge from failure, learning from adjusting strategies and developing solutions based on failure, students can become innovators and be more resilient in their learning. Such ways, I argue, are essential for students as part of a set of understandings and skills needed for work and study as they move to uncertain futures. To be able to fail and learn from this failure could be viewed as a future-proofing skill and may well be a valued capability for future employment. As an educator with long experience working across sectors, it seems to me that developing students' capacities to problem-solve, adapt, experiment, work in solution-oriented groups and exercise agency is ultimately being kind through recognising what they need in times of profound change and allowing them the space to be self-reliant learners. It also promotes qualities such as imagination and courage that are pivotal in being adaptive and creative and making the best in situations of change (Craft et al., 2007).

However, I would not want the reader to get me wrong in my line of argument here. I am not deriding high-stakes testing per se, nor am I ignoring important quantifiable indicators of learning that can be employed holistically as useful measures of success and progress. Measuring growth and development is an important part of what teachers do and assists learners in their understanding of where they are at and what strategies they need to adopt to improve. Such data are also useful for focusing on areas that need attention as teachers and their learners work together.

That is the important point: *to work together* and be a learning community that values every member of that community. I thus argue strongly for the need to bring attention to the relational and the agential in learning, which, at its heart, is about kindness and compassion (Noddings, 2013). I am influenced in this focus by the work of Jewish philosopher Emmanuel Levinas. He has developed a relational ethics which focuses on full recognition of the other in a reciprocal relationship (Levinas, 1969). This, Levinas calls, 'alterity', by which he means the relational in which a person encounters another with full respect, recognition of their independence, genuine interest in who they are, attended by a curiosity, delight, and openness to discovery. According to Levinas, alterity is the necessary basis for compassion and kindness. When students are assigned to categories based on their performance (the A student, the D student), there may be, in my opinion, a loss of compassion and kindness in this categorisation. The assessment and grading of student output should thus be understood holistically in terms of an ethical relationship and encounter.

Dancing with terms: Kindness, creativity, productive failure, agential learning

Before I go further, I want to dance with some key terms that undergird my thinking in this chapter. I engage with these terms definitionally and then ponder their interactions in terms of education. The concepts behind these terms lead to my exploration of an example from my own research practice that embodies kindness, creativity, productive failure and agential learning.

The first term is the notion of kindness. As indicated in Levinas's relational ethics, kindness comes through unfettered recognition of and respect for the other. It is about generosity and often not-asked-for support and consideration in the context of vulnerability or need and a perspective that a student needs more than is offered in the moment that point to growth beyond the immediacy of the classroom. The links to ethical work in all sectors of education are important as educators exercise discernment and courage in understanding and acting towards the needs of students and demonstrating empathy, which is a companion to the act of being kind (Palmer, 2017). A pedagogy of kindness emphasises the fostering of empathy, compassion and supportive learning environments to enhance student wellbeing and holistic growth (Dewey, 1934; Zembylas, 2018).

The second term is *creativity*. The standard definition of creativity is that it is evident in the process of producing something that has novelty (in containing originality) and usefulness in its applications to real-world problems (Runco & Jaeger, 2012). This notion of creativity, however, tends to draw a distinction between individuals quite apart from the context in which creativity emerges. Other research points to creativity as emergent in circumstances and in systems in which learners feel safe and supported and the learning environment is conducive to producing fresh and original work (Beghetto & Kaufman, 2007). So, it is reasonable to assert that kindness is pivotal to the emergence of creativity for students in classrooms. That certainly has been my experience of fostering creativity across all the sectors of education in which I have worked.

A third term related to creativity is *productive failure*. This notion has come to the fore in creativity and educational research in the last several years. Productive failure is an educational approach whereby learners are encouraged to tackle challenging tasks, make mistakes (without fear), and learn from them, fostering deeper understanding and problem-solving skills through reflective experiences (Kapur, 2016). Engaging in productive failure has the potential to develop perseverance and resilience in students.

Finally, agential learning is a process where individuals actively shape their learning experiences, take ownership of their learning journey, and use their personal agency to make critical decisions that influence their knowledge acquisition and skill development (Bandura, 2006). In developing caring learning environments that embody agential learning, educators are using a pedagogy of kindness in allowing learners to find their own way and what works for them without compromising the fundamentals of what students need in order to be successful in work and education beyond school (Noddings, 2012).

I want to go back to my opening discourse to consider how these terms are interrelated. The question for educators with an eye to the future is this: What do our students need for their future? In being kind as educators, students need more than content knowledge (which is often forgotten anyway) and a set of skills, understanding and competencies that will ensure their success in this profound time of change that is likely to continue. The ethical work of the teacher should be about fostering those future-proofing skills, including the ability to be creative, adaptive, resilient and able to learn from failure as a life-long disposition.

A narrative of kindness

In this section, I offer a practice narrative that relates to kindness in the circumstances of a discrete learning context set in a secondary school which was part of a research project. In the first part, I describe the context, the work with participants and what happened for the teacher involved. In the second part, I consider what this narrative suggests about kindness intersecting with risk-taking and productive failure.

Practice narrative from a research project and the Year 8 mathematics teacher

In 2019, I was part of a team that investigated creativity, risk-taking and productive failure in the context of teaching and learning at a private school in Melbourne, Australia. In negotiation with the school, it was decided that Year 8 was the most appropriate level for our investigation. It was clear that the principal of the school was not in favour of any higher level due to expectations from parents about the academic performance of students, which might be compromised by being part of the research. However, he did indicate that this is a progressive school open to innovation and new ideas, and so he believed the research was important.

Most of the Year 8 teachers participated in the study and were enthusiastic about involvement; in fact, we were surprised about just how keen they were and their willingness to try out something new and interrogate their practices. We thus had a good cross section of disciplinary areas represented in our study. We wanted to understand what would happen if learning activities and tasks had an orientation to risk-taking and an increased possibility of failure for students. The research was not overtly about students but about the teachers, their thinking, planning and willingness to be risk-takers. As a research team, we really wanted to value the work and input of the teachers and develop trust as a core value in the research work.

So, we developed a whole-day workshop to prime the teachers, challenge their thinking and give hands-on suggestions for practice and lesson making that incorporated these ideas. It was pleasing to us that the principal and the deputy principal (responsible for the curriculum) of the school attended for the whole day and fully participated in all the activities, working with teachers to integrate risk-taking and productive failure into their pedagogical thinking and the specifics of their curricula. For me, there was an overt kindness from these leaders in supporting their staff through a direct and hands-on approach.

Indeed, there was significant camaraderie on the day that was visceral. Following this workshop, teachers had a 30-day period to enact the principles of risk-taking and productive failure in their classes and it was up to them how these ideas would be instantiated.

We interviewed the teachers before the 30 days to ascertain their outlook and understanding of what we were trying to attain in the research, as well as identifying existing practices that the teachers had already undertaken. There was a second interview at the end of the 30 days that focused on what each teacher did in that 1-month period. There was also a focus group at the end of the 30 days so that teachers could bounce their thoughts off one another in coming to conclusions about what this undertaking meant. Interviews were also conducted with leadership about creativity, risk-taking, productive failure and the possibilities for implementation in that school context. In addition, we developed a Qualtrics-based online journal where teachers could recount their day-to-day experiences of working with risk-tasking and productive failure in their classes.

What was clear from reading and analysing the data is that all the teachers, even those who were reluctant at first, participated in the project because they believed it would shift their practice and develop new learning possibilities for their students. Some of the teachers demonstrated their own risk-taking by doing activities with students that were clearly outside the norm.

I want to focus especially on the experiences of the Year 8 mathematics teacher. In her initial interview with me she expressed some reluctance about trying to implement the concepts of risk-taking and productive failure in mathematics, but, despite reservation, she was willing to give it a go. She admitted that she had never done this sort of thing before and that she predominantly worked within the bounds of the set textbook and the agreed curriculum for the school, which also included the outcomes for mathematics from the Victorian Curriculum. Throughout the 30-day period, she attempted, with varying levels of success, the core research ideas in her daily teaching and learning. This appeared to be a profound experiment for her and she was willing to try because of what she suggested were the important needs of students as they moved forward with their lives. Her passion for the success of her students was clear in all my interactions with her.

One teaching example that she wrote about in her journal and then discussed in the second interview really stood out for me as indicative of the concept of risk-taking and productive failure in concert with a pedagogy of kindness. One lesson she designed was about understanding the mathematical rule for the internal angles of triangles. When the class arrived on the day, she stated that they would not be using their textbooks but doing an activity instead. Around the classroom she had placed different types and shapes of triangles, which she had cut out beforehand and placed in workstations around the classroom. At each workstation, she placed rulers and protractors to facilitate measurement. She introduced the task and explained to students that no textbook or technology could be used. Working in pairs, they should use the instruments provided and come up with the rule.

As the problem-solving task unfolded in the 60-minute lesson, the classroom was noisy as students worked with their partners measuring, writing down possibilities for the rule and changing their minds when it did not work. About 10 minutes into the lesson, some pairs came to the teacher distressed and asked if they could use their textbooks, as they were struggling with the task. There was considerable reticence expressed by some students who protested that this was not the way they had learned mathematics. The teacher explained that the purpose of the task was to find out the mathematical rules for themselves and not rely on the textbook and she encouraged them to explore the possibilities and enjoy their learning. She then sat with the pairs that were struggling and helped them iterate and work through possibilities. What else was happening was that some pairs found the rule quite early and then were helping other pairs also find the rule without giving it away.

Towards the end of the class time, after all the groups had successfully found the rule, some after many tries, she asked one pair who had found it first to report to the whole class. They described their process and what they had found and outlined their steps, including what they did when their first try failed. They also expressed how much they enjoyed the task and said that they wanted more of these types of activities: that it made mathematics interesting.

Reflection through the lens of kindness

At the outset, this research project was framed by a deep respect for the teachers and the school in which it was conducted. We wanted to give back in reciprocity to the school and its educators as much as we gained. I had not reflected on this ethical frame as kindness, but I guess it is. That is perhaps why there was such trust developed between the researchers and the teachers and leaders in the school. We wanted our research to offer some progressive educational ideas which might benefit the school.

The Year 8 mathematics teacher was clearly driven by her concern that her students grow and develop in their mathematical understanding, but the data she offered in this study reveal her deeper concern for equipping her students beyond the confines of her Year 8 mathematics classroom. She evidently has a passion for teaching mathematics; at the same time, she felt the limitations and constraints of how mathematics is typically taught (or at least this is how she described it). That she was willing to take up this more progressive pedagogical approach and engage with productive failure and risk-taking perhaps demonstrates her courage as an educator. Other teachers described how they even flouted some of the policies and practices of the school to enact some of the principles that the researchers had put forward for them to try out. Clearly, not only was there risk-taking by students but also by teachers, as well as courage to see this work through.

In the Year 8 mathematics classroom, the teacher selected a mathematical concept that would have been quite easy to cover by reading the rule in the textbook and indeed, some students preferred it that way, while others were up for the challenge. But driven by her commitment to the research and most especially her desire to see her students be more agential and adopt an approach of discovery, a type of inductive way of constructing knowledge, she soldiered on.

I have four reflections on the kindness that emerged from my consideration of the lesson:

1 The teacher saw the benefit for students in this independent-learning task in making them creative and critical thinkers who iterate and adapt if they fail and are prepared to work towards success. This reinforces their resistance as learners and their willingness to persevere when an immediate solution is not clear.
2 The teacher showed compassion and support for those students who struggled with the task but, at the same time, did not revert to allowing them to use the textbook. In the end, it may be the case that these students who struggled with this open task gained the most benefit.
3 The teacher became an active designer of the learning space such that students could grow through being both challenged and supported in their mathematical learning but, more broadly, about how knowledge is collaboratively created rather than just dispensed.
4 In this classroom, where the teacher gave overt support to the students, they began to support each other without judgement or ridicule.

Implications for education

In the dynamic landscape of education, the concept of a pedagogy of kindness has gained momentum as educators recognise the transformative power of compassion and empathy in the intricacies of the learning process (Noddings, 2012, 2013). When integrated within the contexts of creativity, productive failure and agential learning, this approach can have profound implications, reshaping the educational experience to better meet the needs of students while fostering a supportive and nurturing learning environment (Creely et al., 2021). From my personal reflections from my own research and practice and the practice narrative offered in this chapter, I propose four implications for teaching and learning.

1 *Interconnecting kindness with creativity.* Creativity can be diminished by fear of judgement and failure. It also can flourish in the presence of kindness that drives the foundation of pedagogy. When students feel secure and valued, they are more likely to explore uncharted territories, take risks and think innovatively. A pedagogy of kindness emphasises encouragement over

criticism, allowing learners to express themselves freely without the fear of being reprimanded for unconventional ideas or for trying new approaches that may fail at first. By nurturing creative thinking, educators contribute to the development of problem-solving skills, adaptability and a lifelong love for learning.

2 *Integrating productive failure in learning to grow students.* Productive failure is an essential aspect of the learning journey, as it leads to deeper understanding and resilience, as is clear in the narrative shared previously. In a classroom driven by kindness, failures are treated not as setbacks but as stepping stones to growth in what becomes an inquiry-based approach. Students learn that it is okay to stumble and make mistakes; in fact, it's an integral part of the learning process. This approach shifts the focus of learning from being just about grades to learning as an expansive concept of transformation, encouraging students to analyse their failures, extract meaningful lessons and apply them to future endeavours. The pedagogy of kindness redefines success by valuing the effort, progress and perseverance demonstrated by students, fostering a growth mindset that enhances overall learning outcomes (Zembylas, 2018).

3 *Promoting agential learning.* Agential learning, which pivots learners at the forefront of their educational journey, aligns well with a pedagogy of kindness. By empowering students to make decisions and take responsibility for their learning, educators acknowledge their individuality and autonomy. Kindness in this context involves respecting students' choices, interests, and goals while providing support, guidance and resources to help them navigate their educational path effectively in the short term and long term. This approach not only cultivates self-directed learning skills but also instils a sense of ownership and accountability that can extend beyond the classroom into various facets of life in school and beyond.

4 *Developing a designed and supportive learning environment.* Central to the success of a pedagogy of kindness is the design of a supportive learning environment. This environment goes beyond physical spaces to encompass inferred emotional and psychological spaces as well. It acknowledges the diverse needs and backgrounds of students, catering to their wellbeing and creating a sense of belonging. In a kind classroom, students are more likely to collaborate, offer peer support, and engage in meaningful discussions, enhancing their social skills and emotional intelligence. Teachers can act as facilitators and encouragers, not just disseminators of information or assessors of progress and foster open communication and trust between students and teachers. Moreover, this pedagogical approach addresses the holistic needs of students and recognises the emotions, experiences and challenges learners face.

Emphatically, a pedagogy of kindness has profound implications for education when combined with creativity, productive failure, agential learning and a supportive learning environment. It transforms the classroom into a nurturing space where students are free to explore, make mistakes and grow. This approach equips learners with skills not just for academic success, but social and emotional skills such as empathy, resilience, creativity and self-directed learning. Ultimately, I believe that a climate of kindness in classrooms is a foundation for the capacity building of future generations that not only excel academically but also contribute positively to society.

Conclusion

It is my argument that educators should provide not only the content knowledge required for their students' future but also cultivate qualities like creativity, resilience and adaptability. The ideas of kindness, creativity, productive failure, critical thinking and agential learning explored in this chapter are interwoven and essential for preparing students for an uncertain and rapidly changing world. Pedagogies of kindness are about preparing students for life, not just a narrow set of outcomes and must include strong values such as care, deep support and developing a learning community and environment in which students can be more expansive and expressive in their learning so they can thrive.

In this chapter, I have highlighted the importance of a broadened approach to education, moving beyond just high-stakes testing, quantifiable assessment and content delivery towards kindness, creativity and the willingness to take good risks and learn from failure. I urge educators across all sectors, including those in education, to equip students with lifelong learning skills and engender care in all they do with students. Through the lens of relational ethics, this approach emphasises empathy, respect and innovative problem-solving as keys to future success in times of uncertainty and change. I call for the need to teach students not only how to succeed but how to fail productively, innovate and adapt. The inclusion of a research example from an Australian educational context adds depth and real-world application to my theoretical exploration. I advocate for an education system that is robust, compassionate and fitting for the challenges and opportunities of our time. The realignment of educational goals to emphasise these essential human qualities and needs may well be the key to navigating the profound societal changes ahead.

References

Au, W. (2011). Teaching under the new Taylorism: High-stakes testing and the standardization of the 21st century curriculum. *Journal of Curriculum Studies, 43*(1), 25–45. https://doi.org/10.1080/00220272.2010.521261

Bandura, A. (2006). Toward a psychology of human agency. *Perspectives on Psychological Science, 1*(2), 164–180. https://doi.org/10.1111/j.1745-6916.2006.00011.x

Beghetto, R. A., & Kaufman, J. C. (2007). Toward a broader conception of creativity: A case for "Mini-c" creativity. *Psychology of Aesthetics, Creativity, and the Arts, 1*(2), 73–79. https://doi.org/10.1037/1931-3896.1.2.73

Craft, A., Cremin, T., Burnard, P., & Chappell, K. (2007). Teacher stance in creative arts education: A study of progression. *Thinking Skills and Creativity, 2*(2), 136–147. https://doi.org/10.1016/j.tsc.2007.09.003

Creely, E., Henderson, M., & Henriksen, D. (2019). Failing to succeed: The value of failure in creativity. In K. Graziano (Ed.), *Proceedings of Society for Information Technology & Teacher Education International Conference* (pp. 1403–1411). Las Vegas, NV, United States: Association for the Advancement of Computing in Education (AACE). https://www.learntechlib.org/primary/p/207829

Creely, E., Henriksen, D., Crawford, R., & Henderson, M. (2021). Exploring creative risk-taking and productive failure in classroom practice. A case study of the perceived self-efficacy and agency of teachers at one school. *Thinking Skills and Creativity, 42.* https://doi.org/10.1016/j.tsc.2021.100951

Darling-Hammond, L., & Adamson, F. (2010). *Beyond basic skills: The role of performance assessment in achieving 21st century standards of learning.* Stanford Center for Opportunity Policy in Education.

Dewey, J. (1934). *Art as experience.* Minton, Balch & Company.

Ellis, C., Adams, T. E., & Bochner, A. P. (2011). Autoethnography: An overview. *Forum: Qualitative Social Research, 12*(1), Art. 10. https://doi.org/10.17169/fqs-12.1.1589

Henriksen, D., Creely, E., & Henderson, M. (2019).Failing in creativity: The problem of policy and practice in Australia and the United States. *Kappa Delta Pi Record, 55*(1),4–10. https://doi.org/10.1080/00228958.2019.1549429

Kapur, M. (2016). Examining productive failure, productive success, unproductive failure, and unproductive success in learning. *Educational Psychologist, 51*(2), 289–299. https://doi.org/10.1080/00461520.2016.1155457

Kohn, A. (2000). *The case against standardized testing: Raising the scores, ruining the schools.* Heinemann.

Levinas, E. (1969). *Totality and infinity: An essay on exteriority* (A. Lingis, Trans.). Duquesne University Press.

Noddings, N. (2012). The caring relation in teaching. *Oxford Review of Education, 38*(6), 771–781. https://doi.org/10.1080/03054985.2012.745047

Noddings, N. (2013). *Caring: A relational approach to ethics and moral education* (2nd ed.). University of California Press.

Palmer, P. J. (2017). *The courage to teach: Exploring the inner landscape of a teacher's life.* Jossey-Bass.

Runco, M. A., & Jaeger, G. J. (2012). The standard definition of creativity. *Creativity Research Journal, 24*(1), 92–96. https://doi.org/10.1080/10400419.2012.650092

UNESCO. (2015). *Rethinking education: Towards a global common good?* UNESCO Publishing.

Zembylas, M. (2018). *Re-humanizing pedagogy: Exploring teachers' emotions, empathy, and kindness.* Routledge.

Chapter 8

Black feminism

A pedagogy of radically enacted kindness

Ameena L. Payne and Aris M. Clemons

Introduction

In this chapter, we share stories of how radical kindness has been enacted in our, two Black women scholars', education praxis. First, we draw attention to the fact that "Black teachers' unique historical experiences are [often] either completely overlooked or amalgamated with those of white teachers" (Foster, 1998, p. xlix). As Black women educators and researchers, we believe our role is to build upon and "to preserve what was created before [us]" (Walker, 1984). Therefore, we invoke the social, political and intellectual movement of Black feminism and Black feminist pedagogies (Hill Collins, 1990; hooks, 2015) as we engage the practice of storytelling to reflect on the development of our own pedagogies of kindness. Specifically, we draw on the values of political clarity, inquiry and community as they shape the enactments of radical kindness in both of our, but highlighted in Clemons's, education praxis. Our aim is to challenge dominant narratives that have historically silenced and erased our experiences, while also providing a foundation for building more inclusive and equitable movements for "relational social change" (Perlow et al., 2018, p. 9). As a result, the chapter not only features a conversation between the authors about radical care in our educational practices but also stems from ongoing conversations about reading, writing and learning from and with Black women scholars, mentors, family members and friends. Although we focus on our own experiences as students and teachers, we understand that those experiences cannot be understood outside the collective experiences of those who exist at similar intersections of race, gender and socio-historic contextualisation. As we define care through kindness, we rely on the teachings of all the Black women whom we have had the fortune of encountering during our educational journeys.

We chose to highlight Aris's unique experience given her first-hand experience with Black radical care in her educational development. We began our discussion by probing the ways that our early educational experiences impacted our praxis, beginning with a definition of what it means to care for students with kindness.

DOI: 10.4324/9781003364887-8

For Aris, "caring for [students] means clearing the forest for them." Metaphorically "creating a clearing in the forest" (Foster, 1998, p. 45) means to help someone find a path through a difficult or confusing situation by providing clarity or guidance. Just as a clearing in the forest allows one more visibility, creating a metaphorical clearing can help someone gain a better understanding of their situation to find a way forward and prepare them for life (Foster, 1998). This brand of kindness may involve removing obstacles or providing support. It can also mean creating space for someone to express themselves and be heard. In our conversation, Aris attributed her development of this sense of kindness to her first educational experience in the Nairobi Day School. The Nairobi Day School was a Black-initiated community school created in response to how public schools were failing Black children (Hoover, 1992). The school offered a "skills-oriented curriculum, a caring and community-oriented philosophy, and a pedagogy based on corrective history" (Hoover, 1992, p. 210). She describes this experience, paying close attention to how it impacted her development not only as an educator but also as a language scholar focused on liberatory linguistics (Charity-Hudley et al., 2023).

> So my very first educational experience [was in] what I now call a Black independent Montessori school, and the school is called Shule Ataifa or the Nairobi School … it was very formative … [there were] these women who – and I will tell a story about this really quickly – who were matriarchs and were really taking care of the whole community. Many of these women [involved in the Nairobi Day School] were Black Panthers as well. They were involved in the school lunch programs in Oakland. They later became involved in the Oakland School Ebonics debates which were about giving children the rights to their own languages, and I don't think I fully realised how that was so formative for me until years later. … So having all of these women really centred me in these kinds of Black feminist practices of care, of care for the community, above all, even if it meant fighting against the kind of structural or situational injustices that were happening in our neighbourhoods, in our communities, as well as in our schools. And I took it with me through every single additional educational experience I had.

As Aris continued her pathway toward becoming a Doctor of Philosophy, navigating the challenges and microaggressions of elitist, white academic spaces, she drew on the lessons from her earliest educational experiences, centred on community connectedness, a vision of social justice and kindness. Again, she notes the way that her first educational experience provided her a basis for existing in all spaces, especially those that may be hostile to Black women.

> It doesn't matter what the spaces are. That base that they gave us is there. It allowed you to navigate those spaces and not compromise yourself because you knew [who you were] early on …

Throughout Ameena's upbringing, she was taught to recognise injustice and to always speak up for herself and for others. She was also shown the transformative roles played by ordinary people, by educators and students, as well as the paradoxical roles that the system of education and some of the people within them played in both suppressing and organising for revolution. Her parents came of age during the civil rights movement and they along with other adults in her family, particularly her aunties, embedded in her the importance of and desire to improve educational outcomes for people who have, historically, been denied equal rights and equal opportunities to thrive. It is her belief that a radically kind pedagogy is deliberate and trustworthy; it leads to the open-mindedness to consider a plurality of opinions, respect for others and a boldness to question authority and tradition. Both of our philosophies of kindness require cultivating what we call "a culture of inquiry." In other words, we argue that in order to enact kindness, one must allow others to critically explore themselves and the worlds they occupy.

Fostering a culture of inquiry

The notion of kindness as a pedagogical practice has been gaining more and more traction in educational discourses. In one definition, Denial (2019) notes that as a pedagogical practice, kindness can be simplified as two notions: "believing people and believing in people" (para. 9). In sitting with this provocation, Aris asks:

> But what does that mean in actual practice, right? ... How can you show up for these other human beings in a particular way that are developing their own social consciousness and their own social being?

These notions of pedagogical kindness have little value "without meaningful action and practices" (Willis, 2021, p. 3). We believe one way to move from a theory of kindness to kindness as action is to foster a culture of inquiry, which asks educators to challenge their own beliefs, pedagogies and policies as they engage with every student they encounter. In our conversation, Aris provided an example of how fostering a culture of inquiry can disrupt policies that may not take into consideration the lived experiences of one's students:

> [S]o, you're not only developing a questioner, you're asking questions to get to the core of who your students are, as humans, always. I'll give an example.
>
> When I was an administrator, I had this week where I kept on walking by this classroom every morning at like 8:15 in the morning, and we started school at 7:45, and at 8:15 every morning I was walking by, and this kid, the same kid, was sitting outside this classroom and the door was closed. And they were just sitting there.

And I was like, "[W]hat are you doing here?" And the kid said, you know, the first day the kid was like, "[W]ell, I was late, and the teacher locked the door, and so I was sitting outside."

Okay. One day passed by. The second day passed by and I'm like, "Okay, you were late again." They're like, "yeah." So, I'm like, "What happened?" Like, "Why were you late?" What ended up happening was the child lived in subsidised housing on the other side of the city. In order to get to school by 7:45, they had to leave before the sun came out, and their mom wouldn't let them leave before the sun came out because it wasn't safe. So, they were waiting until the sun came out to leave their house, and they just couldn't make it on time with public transportation. They just couldn't make it on time.

So, then the third day, when they were outside, I knocked on the [classroom] door, and I said, "Did you know that this student was sitting outside?" and the teacher said, "Yes. I knew they knocked on the door and I told them that they couldn't come in because they were late," and I said, "That is a very good rule. Did you ask them why they were late?" and the teacher said, "No." And I said, you know, there's got to be questions no matter what. Even if you decide to apply the policy to the student, you've got to ask the question. You have to know what the student is going through.

In her story, Aris draws on a culture of inquiry as a means to know more deeply the students the teacher is working with. Ameena confirms this notion with her response: "And like you said, it's all about humanising them and understanding their situation and where they're coming from. It's so simple to ask why," to which Aris responded:

It's so simple to ask why, and it's so simple to then become a person who helps to create a solution.

The preceding story demonstrates how kindness is reconceptualised as a radical act of engagement "with those around us to confront oppressive practices in the academy" (Magnet et al., 2014, p. 6) and carceral logics of schooling – such as discipline through humiliation and exclusion (Rudolph, 2023). The idea behind building a culture of inquiry for Ameena rests on both students and educators being encouraged to ask questions, challenge assumptions, and engage in thoughtful interactions (Payne, 2021).

The labour of learning is generative and it "invokes creative and critical thinking [that] widens the horizons … promotes self-reflection, [… and] aims to cultivate a culture of curiosity" (Payne et al., 2022, p. 5); such an approach to assessment also aims to prepare students both within and beyond education. In our conversation, we began to question the very goal of education in modern society. Aris reflected on these goals in speaking about a fundamental learning goal: reading. She asks:

What kind of activities can we get [students] to do to really connect themselves to worlds outside of themselves, to move beyond the cognitive dissonance of your own experience in the world, and to understand that we don't read because we just want to read about ourselves; we also read because we don't have access to things outside of ourselves, and so this gives us access to question the ways that we live our lives. And so, yeah, creating questioners, I think is my teaching philosophy.

A pedagogy centred on kindness requires us to consider how we can incorporate "emotionally actualised teaching" into our approach (Magnet et al., 2014, p. 17). In addition to creating and existing as questioners, we argue that emotionally actualised teaching requires a grounding in socio-political realities. Thus, our second reflection calls on educators to embody political clarity.

Embodying political clarity

We understand education as a deeply personal experience. Furthermore, for people who have been exploited and oppressed, education is, inherently, a matter of politics (hooks, 2015). "From the personal, the striving toward wholeness individually and within the community, comes the political, the struggle against those forces that render individuals and communities unwhole. The personal is political, especially for Black women" (Hull et al., 1995). As such, the Black feminist pedagogy from which we situate our own pedagogies of kindness "flows out of a political commitment" (Henry, 2005, p. 95) and political clarity (Hill Collins, 1990; hooks, 2015). Political clarity involves possessing a clear understanding of one's political beliefs, values and goals as well as a well-defined and coherent perspective on political issues, an understanding of how political systems and institutions operate and who benefits from the ways they are constructed. Although being perceived as "too political" can and has cost Black educators their jobs (Foster, 1998), lived experience has demonstrated that silence does not protect us (Lorde, 1984). Political clarity, particularly in times of political and social upheaval, acts as an orienting tool to help educators remain focused on pursuits and enactments of social justice. Political clarity is something that Aris has engaged in much of her scholarship, her main point being reiterated in our conversation:

There is no action that is not political in the current way that we structure our lives. And so if you're not actually clear about what your political affiliations are, what your alignments are, your goals are, what your motivations are, then you're not actually able to navigate anything, any societal moment, any bit of information, any of your knowledges.

Due to a lack of knowledge of Black and other marginalised students' socio-cultural realities, uncritical educators often position and marginalise students of colour through deficit notions and perceive their roles as educators as help-ing these students overcome their own shortcomings (Foster, 1998) rather than perceiving their students as entering the education environment as "com-plete, complex, undiminished human beings" (Walker, 1984, p. 85). Aris notes this in her experiences with many U.S.-based educators.

> And I've noticed, especially with Black and brown students, because this country [the United States] has a white middle class woman/female-presenting teaching populace that often what happens in those spaces is that the students get coddled in a way that becomes not caring and unkind, and it becomes a situation where the reason why teachers are coddling them is because there's a deep belief that students are not capa-ble of doing things.

Coddling is a form of deficit thinking that sustains the belief that non-white students are inherently less capable or have less potential than their white peers (Foster, 1998). White teachers may engage in coddling behaviour when they lower their expectations of non-white students and shield them from chal-lenges that they perceive as being too difficult (Foster, 1998). This brand of "kindness" has been and continues to be performed as an "act of benevo-lence" – a way in which white educators "construct themselves in relation to their others" (Willis, 2021, p. 5). The issue of coddling and deficit thinking around non-white students' capabilities are not just educational issues but also political ones. Given that educational institutions are situated within what we call the Judeo-Christian white supremacist capitalist patriarchal structures, "feeling kind is not enough" (Magnet et al., 2014, p 6). Kindness is enacted and it is political (Willis, 2021). Thus, by embodying political clarity, we actively combat deficit thinking through our own self-reflection.

Teaching from a Black feminist perspective illuminates radical kindness as a micropolitical and pedagogical strategy which serves to benefit all students. The empowerment that may be fostered for both students and educators alike reflects a style of activism and a belief in self-reliance and self-determination (Hill Collins, 1990). A pedagogy founded on Afrocentric values illuminates that teaching is not equivalent to "telling" and requires educators to be more self-critical (Foster, 1998). In her own self-critique, Aris examines why she works as an educator:

> Most likely people are like, well, we have to get [students] to a certain benchmark. They have to learn a certain amount of things. And so they're collecting facts like collectibles. We have this idea that education is meant to fill these receptacles with a certain amount of content, but I definitely don't feel like that. And so my overarching understanding and desire for education is to give students the tools to be able to think critically and to examine the world around them critically – to be able to manage for

themselves the ways that they navigate the world in ways that will allow them to do so healthily, like with any kind of like mental stability and protection against the bullshit that is life.

The value of knowledge lies in its practical application (Foster, 1998). Black feminist pedagogy can unmask "the complexities of teaching in counter-hegemonic and transgressive ways such as trying to articulate alternative visions along with students" (Henry, 2005, p. 95). In thinking about practical applications of political clarity, Aris reflects on the complexities of holding political beliefs that may be incongruent with the beliefs of many students in her teaching context:

> Right now, I'm in a southern context. I'm in Knoxville [Tennessee, USA] which means that, though my own political beliefs are quite progressive, some might say radically so, I may not be in the presence of a bunch of radical progressive students. I bring this up because my conservative leaning [students] ... um, I would say that, you know, they're still Gen Z so they still have a different level of conservatism ...
>
> They are often fearful in their college classes, in our college classes, and knowing, especially when they walk into the room and they're like, "Okay, this is a Black female teacher like she's probably liberal," you know what I mean? And I've become quite close with quite a few of them. Many of my colleagues are like, "How are you dealing with the conservative kids?" and I was like, "I'm letting them question themselves out of their own beliefs." I am not challenging their beliefs – I mean, I challenge their beliefs by making them ask questions to themselves and really think critically about where they got their ideas from, who benefits from their ideas, who may not benefit from their ideas, who may benefit from the construction of their ideas in a particular way? What happens if they switch it up? Like all of those kinds of things.
>
> And so, I never say no, you're wrong. I don't think I've ever said that to a student. I have asked them to ask more questions. I have given them the tools to determine which questions are answerable through different methodologies, which questions are not answerable through current ways of thinking about established problems.

Responding to Aris's comments on dealing with political incongruencies, Ameena notes, "Educators are often told to be apolitical, and that's not setting students up to be in-the-world, is it?" To this, Aris responded:

> Like at all ... it's actually a little bit weird because ... it's the opposite ... it's setting people up to be in the world in a particular way ... my teaching philosophy is to create thinkers and questioners, right, people who are critically thinking and questioning the world around them, constantly questioning

their own positionality and questioning the ways that they're interacting with the world as they move through different contexts. …

That's not safe for capitalism. That's not safe for imperialism. That's not safe for white supremacy. And so, the system of education is the antithesis of Black teaching and Black pedagogy. Black teaching and Black pedagogy are not safe for the current system as it exists.

Conversely, political apathy is often championed in the corporate university as a means to continue "educating for domination" (hooks, 2015, p. 101). We challenge education for the purpose of domination and instead suggest kindness as a way to build connectedness through community.

Connectedness through community

Engaging students as co-conspirators

We engage as educators in ways that reflect the reality that our students "could one day grow up and be [our] neighbors" (Foster, 1998, p. 61). We further engage with students as they progress through varying stages of academic training as if they could one day be our colleagues, which Aris describes through her notion of co-conspirators:

This is also what I've learned about enacting pedagogies of kindness: that even though your administration and the institutions that you work with may be structured by ideologies of white supremacy, if you are serving a particular population, then that is who you engage. That is who becomes your co-conspirators. Those are the people that, because that's who you're serving, and that's who you care about anyway, then they become the people that fight alongside you.

Herein, we take up Willis's (2021) assertion that "kindness requires companions: commitment to justice, critical (and self-critical) acuity, affirmation of equity" (p. 6). Kindness also requires relationality, reciprocity, vulnerability, openness and love. Importantly, Aris challenges unkind distancing techniques often reinforced through notions of professionalism by challenging educators to personalise their relationships with their students:

I am often shocked by the amount of misanthropes that I find in this field. I remember when I was an administrator, I had several conversations, and we ended up having PDs [professional development] on loving children like they were your own. It was very interesting because when you say that a lot of times people think that that means that they really have to treat these kids as if they were their own children, which means a lot of that negative behaviour that I was talking about in terms of coddling.

And so they had a hard time holding kids accountable when you just said "love them like they're your own child," and so I started to instead share with my colleagues what does it mean to love somebody and to care for a human being as if they were going to be your boss? What does it mean to care for somebody as if they were going to be your collaborator, as if they were going to be your co-conspirator and work alongside you to achieve a particular goal?

What would you want from them? What kind of human being would you want them to be? Would you want them to also have grace? Would you have grace for them? Would you want them to have grace for you, right? And how do you train them to do these things, right?

Shifting our perspective from risk to possibilities is essential in how we perceive others and the ways we portray kindness. Ameena's idea of kindness emphasises the importance of subverting pathologisation. Emphasising the humanity of herself and others, Ameena foregrounded radical kindness through innovating how she engaged in feedback with students which she discusses in Rossi's (2023) book on inclusive learning design. This was a move that emphasised relationality and challenged the discursive and prescriptive boundaries that shape and uphold the conservative traditions of education.

Aris: When we're talking about black feminist praxis, we think of bell hooks and we think about love, right? We think of Patricia Hill Collins, and we think of drawing the margins into the centre. We think of Angela Davis, and we think of standing up for those who don't have rights, right? Like your job is not to just know a bunch of facts and then spew those facts at kids.

Engaging the community as allies

Black feminism posits that individuals can only achieve a sense of humanity and empowerment within community by actively seeking connections, interactions and relationships that promote harmony (Hill Collins, 1990). Brought up with the notion of being and becoming our "selves-in-community" (Moore & Billingsley, 2017, p. 245), we recall our individual uniqueness often taught to us by our maternal figures (Walker, 1984). The concept of being grounded in and accountable to community is central to Black women's (and our) construction of knowledge. Aris reflects:

I think that in education, in academia, in the current society that we live in, people want answers, and they want that to be simple. "Tell me what to do and I will do it." And I think that also has to do with the way education has been structured over the last 50 years, and that the fact that we haven't been being trained to be thinkers and to find solutions and things like that, but almost always things are not as simple as you think they are, and almost always no solution is going to work unless it's community driven from the context that you're coming from.

And so my advice in that case is to become integrated in the communities that you become an educator in, in some way, so that doesn't mean that I'm saying to work at your soup kitchen every weekend or, you know, do these kinds of, like, different moments of activism.

That means if you are really into Dungeons and Dragons, then you start a community club. That means that you ask questions about your community … you ask people what they want. And it also very much means that even though you have a level of education and you have a level of a certain style of living that maybe some of your students may not have, that you don't assume that that means that you know more what they need than they know what they need, right?

And so oftentimes, communities know exactly what they want and need to solve their problems and don't have the resources or the bridges to be able to do those things and that is where we can come in as educators. That is where we can come in as human beings that have access to knowledge about how to get more resources. And that is what we provide. We don't provide them with telling them what they need for themselves.

Conclusion

Pedagogies of kindness are vital during times of political upheaval as they may better enable us to navigate challenging circumstances. Thus, prompting the need to examine the ways in which we build and sustain relationships and partnerships (Costello, 2022). When thinking about the concept of radical kindness, Costello (2022) asks, "How can educators, who wish to adopt a critically reflexive stance, respond to this? Or rather where can they respond from?" (p. 2). To this Aris responded:

> You know the craziest thing is we've just come out of this very intense moment of pandemic and intense turmoil, emotionally, physically. I mean, students were losing family members, getting ill, you know … at a time where they are learning about who they are as people, developing their own personalities, developing their own political praxis, like all of those kinds of things are happening all at the same time …
>
> So, I think for me, enacting a pedagogy of radical kindness is to put at the forefront and to centre the humanity of every single student, every single individual student first, not what they can produce in a capitalistic society, not in a neoliberal way of creating, or this idea that education is meant to create a productive citizen. I don't actually subscribe to that. I actually

believe that caring for and developing a person's humanity in a way that they deem fit is most important, and so what that means is that I often have to shift my pedagogical practices every time I enter into a new space with a new group of students …

And so, I had to … not give a shit about what they were supposed to be doing or producing for a particular class. So, one of the things that I started to tell myself and to think about was, "what is the one core message you want every student to take away from this course?"

Radical kindness is not just about how we can serve our students within a given institutional context but also about how we can better serve ourselves and recognise our own humanity. Importantly, Aris is advocating for models that privilege the humanity of educators as a way to centre the humanity of our students:

[Educators] get to have moments of humanity as well; they get to be frustrated, and that means that they need to learn how to ask for help and advocate for themselves in the same way that they advocate for their students.

So, if they find themselves in a moment where they are struggling to find the humanity in their students, then they ask for help, and they're honest about that, and hopefully they have administrators that are also responsive to them as human beings, right? I often say students don't fail teachers; teachers fail students. Teachers don't fail students, administrators fail teachers. Administrators don't fail teachers; states fail administrators and so on.

I think the core of it [is] really: find ways to find humanity in your students, in what you're doing and also in yourself.

Teaching is a profession rooted in ethics – it's a moral craft that tugs at our hearts, values, and energy, just like any other moral calling. It's not just about being a good teacher or creating a socially just classroom in isolation; we're talking about rolling up our sleeves and diving into the vibrant tapestry of the larger community. It is a challenging task that necessitates safeguarding and fostering our own well-being.

Embracing Black feminism as the foundation of our pedagogy has empowered us to nurture a culture of inquiry, cultivate and embody political clarity, and forge deep connections in community. Let us commit to actively engaging with these principles, amplifying the stories, experiences and pedagogies of Black women, and working towards a kinder society for all.

Acknowledgements

We would like to express our sincere gratitude to Dr. Cathy Stone for sharing the opportunity to contribute to this book; her decision to share this opportunity is a testament to her commitment to creating more diverse and inclusive spaces within academia.

References

Charity Hudley, A. H., Clemons, A. M., & Villarreal, D. (2023). Language across the disciplines. *Annual Review of Linguistics, 9*, 253–272.

Costello, E. (2022). Rewild my heart: With pedagogies of love, kindness and the sun and moon. *Postdigital Science and Education.* https://doi.org/10.1007/s42438-022-00318-z

Denial, C. (2019, August 15). A pedagogy of kindness. *Hybrid Pedagogy.* https://hybridpedagogy.org/pedagogy-of-kindness/

Foster, M. (1998). *Black teachers on teaching.* https://thenewpress.com/books/black-teachers-on-teaching

Henry, A. (2005). Chapter four: Black feminist pedagogy: Critiques and contributions. *Counterpoints, 237*, 89–105.

Hill Collins, P. (1990). *Black feminist thought: Knowledge, consciousness, and the politics of empowerment.* Unwin Hyman.

hooks, b. (2015). *Talking back: Thinking feminist, thinking black.* Routledge.

Hoover, M. E. R. (1992). The Nairobi Day School: An African American independent school, 1966–1984. *The Journal of Negro Education, 61*(2), 201–210. https://doi.org/10.2307/2295416

Hull, A., Bell-Scott, P., & Smith, B. (1995). *But some of us are brave: A history of Black feminism in the United States.* https://racism.org/articles/intersectionality/gender/2281-but-some-of-us-are

Lorde, A. (1984). *Sister outsider: Essays and speeches.* Crossing Press.

Magnet, S., Mason, C. L., & Trevenen, K. (2014). Feminism, pedagogy, and the politics of kindness. *Feminist Teacher, 25*(1), 1–22. https://doi.org/10.5406/femteacher.25.1.0001

Moore, G. C., & Billingsley, A. (2017). *Maternal metaphors of power in African American women's literature: From Phillis Wheatley to Toni Morrison.* The University of South Carolina Press.

Payne, A. L. (2021). A resource for e-moderators on fostering participatory engagement within discussion boards for online students in higher education. *Student Success, 12*(1), Article 1. https://doi.org/10.5204/ssj.1865

Payne, A. L., Ajjawi, R., & Holloway, J. (2022). Humanising feedback encounters: A qualitative study of relational literacies for teachers engaging in technology-enhanced feedback. *Assessment & Evaluation in Higher Education*, 1–12. https://doi.org/10.1080/02602938.2022.2155610

Perlow, O. N., Wheeler, D. I., Bethea, S. L., & Scott, B. M. (2018). *Black women's liberatory pedagogies: Resistance, transformation, and healing within and beyond the academy.* Springer International Publishing.

Rossi, V. (2023). *Inclusive learning design in higher education: A practical guide to creating equitable learning experiences.* Taylor & Francis Group.

Rudolph, S. (2023). Carceral logics and education. *Critical Studies in Education*, 1–18. https://doi.org/10.1080/17508487.2022.2153373

Walker, A. (1984). *In search of our mothers' gardens: Womanist prose.* Women's Press.

Willis, E. (2021). Editorial: Performance and radical kindness. *Performance Paradigm*, (16), Article 16.

Chapter 9

Leading with heart, authenticity and insight

The (hard) work of enacting kindness across an institution

Tim Moss

Introduction and context

In this chapter, I provide a narrative account of one higher education institution's development of a 'kind' culture, one that emphasises heart, authenticity and insight as fundamental principles of teaching, learning and working together. I trace the early work that enabled us to arrive at a shared understanding of who we were as an institution and what we stood for and then the challenges and disruptions that have allowed us to test the borders, stress points and foundations of this understanding. Ultimately, this is a narrative of our growth as an institution, alongside my own personal growth as a leader who endeavours to act with integrity, empathy and kindness.

To begin this account, I must start with an observation that I have both heard and expressed many times of late: kindness is harder now.

When I started at the Australian College of the Arts (Collarts) in 2019, in a newly created role as Associate Dean eLearning and Innovation, I was immediately struck by a feeling that I had arrived somewhere that was ... different. Different from the university environments that I had worked in previously, large, clumsy behemoths of things where it wasn't always clear who everyone in the staff room was, why they were there, or what we were supposed to be achieving.

At Collarts, we were (and still are) small. We are focused. As a non-university provider, we can be; we don't need to offer courses in every discipline. Indeed, we don't; our focus is wholly and solely creative industries courses. We can also be quite clear on our purpose; we exist to provide students with pathways to creative careers and/or personal and professional actualisation and fulfilment, provide our connected industries with a new generation of creative professionals and perhaps, just a little bit, show that there are alternatives to the university-style 'mass education' model, with our small class sizes and emphasis on knowing our students as people. Also, as a non-university provider, our purpose is narrowed for us; there's no specific requirement for our teachers or indeed our institution as a whole to engage in research activity (although scholarship, defined more broadly, is required) and we can't receive

DOI: 10.4324/9781003364887-9

any research grant income. So, we are there for students, teaching and engaging with industry.

All of this really leads back to my feeling of arriving somewhere different. There was a sense of coherence, clarity and shared effort; with a singular focus on teaching and students, it felt as though everyone was pushing in the same direction. There were long conversations about student experience, how we could support students through all kinds of difficulties and how we could make their first experience of study more engaging and meaningful. It was exciting, promising and different. Our teaching team was relatively young, mostly new to higher education, but keen to make up for any lack of teaching experience through enthusiasm, positivity and an extended repertoire of stories from their time in industry.

Building the culture

It's important to acknowledge that, of course, this culture hadn't developed by accident. After a period of some moderate upheaval, the Dean had led a significant piece of work, supported by external coaching and consultancy, to develop and articulate a set of shared values that could work to unite the organisation. These values had been 'launched' with great success about a year before my arrival and it wasn't at all uncommon for me to hear staff referring to 'The Collarts Way' values, which included being student-centric, passionate, authentic and professional. Sometimes, after a particularly challenging period or after resolving a complex situation, staff members would receive a 'Collarts Way Shout Out', whereby a colleague would describe what this individual had done, the impact of that, and which Collarts Way values this modelled. I think most of us let out a (very small) groan whenever a 'Collarts Way Shout Out' appeared in our email inbox, because it would almost immediately be met by several dozen 'reply all' responses, full of supportive comments and congratulations. I hadn't encountered anything like this before, and it took me a while to 'tune in' to this culture and the positivity it seemed to engender for our mission, our culture and each other.

In that context, it was easy to be kind and to lead for kindness.

The Dean and I were keen to explore how we could expand the enthusiasm people held for the Collarts Way. At that time, it was a powerful tool for giving coherence and context to how our staff felt about their work and each other, but it didn't really provide them with any clarity in terms of what they could, or should, actually do in their roles. We wanted to take this values-based culture and find a way to build on it in order to define an academic approach, a teaching framework. And that task primarily fell to me.

Across the next six months (between mid-2019 and early 2020), we planned and implemented a whole-of-community process of reflection, discussion and critique aimed at identifying and codifying the values, dispositions and practices that best captured what was at the core of our teaching approach as an organisation. This process involved workshops, individual conversations, student surveys and whole-of-staff seminars to analyse and interpret what our community valued about teaching and learning. This process relied upon several assumptions that I made, about how such a framework would best be created and owned.

The first of these was that we should start with students. Knowing that being 'student-centric' was a core aspect of the existing Collarts Way and knowing also that we had a small and highly engaged student body, I felt that student voice would serve to unify our purpose and give our staff something concrete to engage with. Through focus groups and student surveys, all Collarts students had the opportunity to tell us, "What makes a great Collarts teacher", and identify the things that were important to them as learners. Synthesising their responses provided a series of 'provocations' that teachers were then invited to respond to – statements such as "a great Collarts teacher knows what I want, and what I am afraid of", and "a great Collarts teacher makes me feel safe to be myself".

The second assumption that guided this process was that we should listen to all voices. Following the process of gathering student 'provocations', I facilitated a series of workshops with a wide range of staff, gathering their observations, insights and questions in relation to what students had identified. We used a variety of applications and tools to support this process, which meant that we could quickly synthesise and further reflect on our shared insights and ensured that all participants had an equal voice and equal representation.

The third assumption guiding this process was the importance of making it real. By this I mean ensuring that discussions remained grounded in practice; as we began to draw out overarching principles and elements of practice, it was important that we could identify not just why these sounded like nice things to value but also what they meant for what we would actually do. If we identified a value that sounded appropriate but we couldn't articulate what that would actually mean in terms of putting that value into practice, we removed it. We already had the Collarts Way to guide us in how we felt; what we were building here needed to guide what we did.

As the framework began to take shape, we held all-staff professional development sessions where we asked 'champions' of practice to describe situations that embodied particular principles (e.g. what did it look like to provide a 'safe' learning environment) and then invited others to share their own examples. Through that process, we were able to identify some principles that sounded great but were not particularly helpful or specific, and these were either refined or discarded. These workshops became a powerful tool for inviting ownership of our process and indeed our framework, as participants were essentially learning about the framework whilst at the same time learning through the framework.

In later workshops, we reviewed early drafts of the framework, exploring ways of phrasing particular principles and elements that resonated with participants across a variety of roles (including teachers, leaders and students). These sessions frequently became the sites of intense conversations about which words and concepts best described what we really meant (e.g. should we say that we teach with heart, or should we say that we teach with care – and what might be the differences between these?).

The end result of these refining workshops was a values-based teaching framework that we deliberately called the Collarts Way of Teaching. We wanted this framework to both reference and build on the Collarts Way, showing that for our organisation, it was important that we could articulate and embody the values that underpinned our practice. Figure 9.1 is an 'at-a-glance' visual representation of the final framework.

This extended process of consultative development meant that by the time we reached this final version, many across the organisation already felt they understood it and that it described an approach that they owned and valued. There was a sense of pride in the final outcome, as teachers in particular felt that it gave prominence and voice to key elements of their practice. In the context of exploring kindness, it is perhaps interesting to note that the most consistently identified aspect of the framework that resonated with many individuals was the notion of teaching with heart. Coming from the university context described at the start of this chapter, this was something of a revelation for me – here I found myself in a place where staff not only claimed to be student-centric but were also actively connecting their practice to empathy, compassion and inclusivity.

In a similar way to the Collarts Way Shout Outs that had made such an impact on the culture prior to the development of this framework, we began to see teachers sharing examples of practice that they had seen or heard from their colleagues that demonstrated being person-centred, or promoting active learning, or modelling great partnerships.

One such example that still resonates with me today relates to a challenging situation between a student and a sessional teacher who had been very actively engaged in developing the framework. This teacher had needed to reschedule a class at short notice and had contacted the students via email to let them know. One student, who had previously presented some challenging behaviours in class, wrote a scathing 'reply all' email about how dissatisfied he was with the class to date, including some extremely colourful language to describe the teacher. One of the other students was so shocked by this email that they forwarded it to the Head of Department. Clearly, the 'reply all' email was a breach of the code of conduct. In most other organisations I've worked, the student would have been reported and some form of penalty imposed. In this case, however, a different outcome ensued.

First, the Head of Department checked in with the teacher to ensure that they were feeling okay and see what they felt the next step should be.

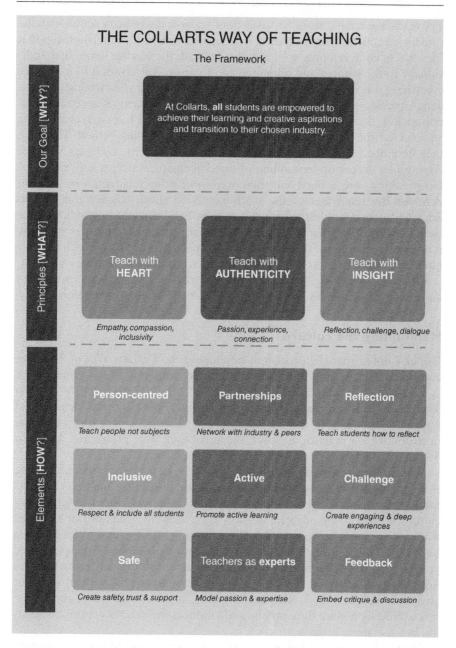

Figure 9.1 An 'at a glance' visual representation of the framework.

The teacher asked if it would be okay not to pursue disciplinary action with the student, as this behaviour seemed very inconsistent with the relationship that they had been developing to this point. Instead, the teacher wrote back individually to the student and organised an in-person conversation to make sure everything was okay and discuss what had happened. At the meeting, the student expressed remorse for sending the email in a moment of anger and frustration and then described some aspects of the unit that had been challenging and had left the student feeling as though they were falling behind. Together, they developed a study plan that would help the student re-engage with the class, gain a deeper understanding of the challenging concepts and 'catch up'. No penalties were applied and there were no further incidents with the student for the remainder of the teaching period. Both teacher and student described how valuable they felt this process had been and how different the outcome was from what they anticipated might have happened. To me, there is no clearer example of the value of taking a person-centred approach to every interaction with students and taking seriously the notion of teaching with heart.

Of course, finalising the framework was only the start of the process of ensuring that we owned and adopted it across the whole organisation.

Maintaining the culture

Earlier I noted that the process of developing the Collarts Way of Teaching concluded in early 2020. At this point, we had 'launched' the final framework at a whole staff professional development event, we had started to develop some exemplars and case studies to support each principle and element and staff were beginning to use the language of the framework in their conversations about their practice. In short, the initial signs were promising. And then March 2020 happened, and with it, COVID-19.

Whilst this narrative is not about the COVID-19 pandemic, it is fair to note that the pandemic caused significant change and disruption and that our plans for how we would use the Collarts Way of Teaching to further strengthen our culture needed to be adapted to meet the changing needs of our staff and students. It is also fair to note that these changes and disruptions are far from resolved; if there is one key learning from our experience of the past three years as an educational institution, it is that there is simply no 'going back' to how things used to be. To survive in this new, uncertain context, different attributes were required. Resilience was key, as were adaptability and persistence. Finding a place for empathy and kindness was certainly more challenging but also more important.

Alongside enforced changes to how and where we could teach, we experienced a number of structural changes through the COVID-19 period. Surprisingly, our student numbers grew rapidly, to the point where we moved from a relatively flat academic structure to a school-based structure, meaning the introduction of heads of school and a greater 'distance' between teaching teams and academic leadership. We developed and launched a wide range of new courses, meaning that our teaching teams were also expanding, with new teachers and course leaders needed. We spent several teaching periods with all classes held online and remotely and then several more with semi-frequent interruptions to delivery caused by changing health restrictions before finally settling into a pattern of online, on-campus and some hybrid delivery. We ramped up our wellbeing support for students (and staff) who were struggling with isolation, anxiety, and challenging economic situations. And in the midst of these challenges, I moved to the role of Dean, taking on a broader set of responsibilities around academic leadership, strategy, and human resource management.

It is impossible to know how the Collarts Way of Teaching might have shaped our institution in a different context. In the COVID-19 context, it certainly provided a signpost for the direction in which we had decided we would move. However, the signpost was not a map, and as we encountered new challenges and obstacles, we found it to be more or less useful, more or less central, as our destination kept shifting and as our party of travellers changed shape and composition. In a sense, I suspect this is the challenge with any attempt to create meaningful change (even, as in our case, when the majority of stakeholders actually embrace that change), in that the set of skills and processes that help you to build the plan are not always the same as those needed to enact and sustain it.

For me, maintaining our culture and enacting the Collarts Way of Teaching was first and foremost a case of modelling. If I (and the institution) felt that this framework was accurate in describing what we valued about the ways in which we worked with each other, then it was essential that my peers and colleagues be able to see it in my practice. I worked to find ways of leading with heart, authenticity and insight.

Leading with heart sounds simple, and in many ways it is; it meant taking care of the person with whom I was interacting and attending to their wider needs, motivations and goals. It meant finding ways to create inclusive and safe spaces for staff, which often meant being very clear that I was someone who would always listen without judgement and who would be available. In situations of conflict or tension, this meant modelling the same process of seeking first to understand that the teacher demonstrated in the example I provided earlier, recognising that all behaviour has logic to those performing it.

Leading with authenticity is for me about recognising the privilege of my position and ensuring I frame my experiences and interactions from a place of passion, experience and connection. It is about viewing all colleagues as partners, finding ways to bring people together to recognise and achieve shared goals and ensuring that I deliver what I say I will. A key aspect of my approach is an emphasis on dialogic decision-making, ensuring that issues are discussed, options explored and then consensus achieved (to the extent that is possible).

Finally, leading with insight is about recognising the importance of feedback and reflection. As a leader, I had long struggled with 'people pleasing', emphasising the attainment of a positive or 'nice' outcome even over the clarity or efficacy of that outcome. I had avoided conversations that had the potential to become uncomfortable or challenging, thinking that this was not a 'kind' way to be a leader. However, that approach is, in reality, incompatible with clear and insightful leadership. My challenge has been to find ways to provide feedback, challenges and critiques that are kind while at the same time lead to change and improvement. I have had to recognise that challenge and tension are often prerequisites for change and growth, that feedback is only useful if it is clear and specific, and that it is sometimes not possible to avoid short-term discomfort in the service of long-term improvement. The connections established in the Collarts Way of Teaching between reflection, dialogue and insight have been highly influential and the hardest parts for me to model as a leader through this period.

A challenging context

It's important to note that implementing this new framework didn't take place in a perfect or 'controlled' environment. Rather, the context in which we operated, both within and beyond our institution, meant that a number of challenges presented themselves and continue to do so. These challenges continue to test not only the Collarts Way of Teaching framework but also the fundamental principles and beliefs of our organisation. These are challenges to how we work together, what we value, what we believe and who we are. When confronted with challenges of this nature, leading with kindness becomes harder.

The first such challenge was staff turnover. In a period of rapid growth, we found ourselves needing to set up whole departments and course teams multiple times a year and ensure that we were scaling our support systems and processes to match. For the first two years of our new framework, we were also doing this almost entirely remotely, with frequent and sustained lockdowns and restrictive health measures, meaning there was little to no scope to bring people together. If it is difficult to build a shared culture with everyone together, it is even harder to manage this when there is no opportunity for ad hoc conversations or the kind of problem-solving and collaboration that occur simply by being in the same space as colleagues. To overcome this, we worked hard to develop our online systems and processes and continued to offer whole-staff professional development sessions through synchronous online platforms.

Alongside the growth in teams, as restrictions eased, we saw a number of staff members move on from Collarts. The result of these ongoing ebbs and flows in our staff community was a feeling that we were forever starting again; while we developed effective induction processes to introduce the framework, we were seemingly forever 'stuck' at this introductory step, with no free resources to work with our experienced staff and 'go deeper' into the implications of our teaching framework.

A second challenge, which is somewhat more intangible to identify and manage as a leader, was a growing sense of fatigue within our teams. What began with one teaching period of 'emergency remote teaching' continued through several years of interruption, restriction, and a continual need to adapt and respond to an uncertain external environment. And the reality is that it is hard to sustain an 'emergency' response over that time. With too many variables to control and too many changes to respond to, we began to see signs of 'decision fatigue', a slowing pace of adaptation and eventually a growing sense of exhaustion, weariness and burnout. There was little time for reflection, especially for shared conversations and solutions and it all began to feel like too much. Collarts Way Shout Outs became fewer and further between; situations of complex tension (such as student and staff complaints), although still infrequent, began to increase. For the first time since I had started at Collarts, we were dealing with human resources matters, such as underperformance and minor conduct issues. This meant difficult conversations, with specific protocols to be followed, which didn't always seem to present the space for kindness to be a guiding principle.

As these signs of fatigue began to present across the institution, we also found ourselves dealing with expectations from students that seemed to be increasingly challenging to meet. Students who had completed several years of their schooling from their bedrooms were presenting as uncertain of themselves, intolerant of ambiguity and unwilling to take risks in their learning, particularly of the kind that are fundamental to effective arts education. Teachers reported finding it difficult to engage these students, not just in deepening their learning but even in basic actions such as attending class and submitting assessments. In an environment where we had emphasised empathy and heart as fundamental aspects of the Collarts Way of Teaching, teachers experienced these challenges both personally and professionally.

With students seemingly so confronted by the notion of change or uncertainty, teachers were becoming more reluctant to take risks in their practice for fear of further disengagement. In a contemporary higher education context, where students are seen (and often treated) as 'customers', it was becoming apparent that they had taken this treatment to heart and expected a learning experience that was safe, comfortable and presented entirely on their terms. Furthermore, they were making choices about how to engage with study that prioritised their 'lives' over their learning, as has been reported elsewhere in the literature on post-pandemic student engagement (Hews et al., 2022). While it's beyond the scope of this chapter to explore how we have worked to address these challenges to engagement, it is essential to note that the way students engage with us has a direct and significant implication for how our teachers, support staff and leaders feel about themselves, their role and their capacity to act with empathy and kindness.

Addressing the challenges

In the context of these challenges, leading with kindness is more important and potentially also more difficult. I feel it's important to note at this point that I don't have a 'conclusion' to this narrative. I haven't found the solution, solved the problems, or found a simple recipe for others to follow. What I have done is tried, failed, and iterated and through that process, I've found some ways to move forward, tentatively, with kindness as a guiding principle.

The first such technique that has proven effective in addressing these challenges and leading with kindness is to build 'kind systems' and processes. By this I mean analysing all staff-facing policies and processes, to ensure that these reflect post-pandemic realities in higher education and identify what success might look like in that context. For example, in late 2023, we rewrote our academic staff progression policy (the process through which academic staff receive 'promotion' and increased remuneration), away from a focus on out-of-context outcomes (e.g. student survey results above a certain level) and towards a focus on process (e.g. evidence of actions taken, successful or otherwise, in response to student surveys). This opens up space for teachers to take more risks and replace tried-and-tested, and stale, pedagogical approaches with newer approaches, even when it takes time to refine these processes or bring tentative, risk-averse students 'on board'. We do this as a way of building trust into our systems, showing that, following Denial (2019), we believe people and believe in people, not just in our interactions with them but in the very way we define success and achievement at an organisational level. By adopting a systemic approach, we also build in a way to ensure that new starters are quickly brought up to speed with our fundamental values.

The second technique that has been instrumental in leading for kindness in a challenging context is to adopt dialogic processes in decision-making and in as many interactions as possible. To achieve this, we hold regular meetings with key stakeholder groups, including permanent staff employed as academic leaders, permanent teaching staff and our group of casual teachers. These meetings are held with deliberately open agendas so that all participants can raise any items of concern for discussion and review. These meetings are supported with asynchronous collaborative tools, including the use of Teams for group conversation and collaboration and Miro for recording notes and decisions and to enable further reflection and development of ideas. Establishing a regular cadence for conversations, and a shared agenda, means that these become opportunities for responsive leadership. Where issues are raised, I attempt to emphasise process when finding a resolution: how might we work together to resolve this, who might we need to consult, how will we know we've achieved success. In this way, my intention is never just to resolve a situation; rather, it is to empower individuals, create agency and encourage empathy through interaction and dialogue. This also means that our approach is rarely dependent on any one individual to succeed, which, in turn, helps overcome fatigue, as individuals can 'take a breath' and know that others will be there to support and ensure projects and actions can be continued.

Finally, and this technique sounds deceptively simple, as a leader I make a conscious and sustained effort to create a culture where we call out kindness with kindness. Where students achieve wonderful things, we acknowledge not just the student but also the teachers who supported them to achieve it. Where acts of kindness are observed, we continue to call these out through all-staff Collarts Way Shout Outs, probably the only 'reply all' email we encourage. Where student feedback highlights effective or innovative practice, we ask teachers of these units to share insights, techniques and resources through communities of practice. And where these effective practices are sustained over time, we support the teachers involved to consolidate and share their practice more formally, for example through a mentoring program that culminates in submission of an application for an Advance HE fellowship at the appropriate level.

At a personal level, I try to keep heart, authenticity and insight at the core of my interactions and often find that active listening is the most effective way to achieve this. In listening before speaking, I am resisting adversarial positions (Denial, 2019) and remaining focused on the person in the situation. Of course, I don't always succeed, and outcomes are not always positive, much as new pedagogical approaches don't always match our anticipated outcomes the first time they are employed. And in this, I also need to be kind to myself, to recognise that it's only really through experience that we can improve our capacity to achieve the outcomes we are aiming for.

Kindness is hard

In reflecting on my practice as a leader, I have experienced many moments of doubt and uncertainty. Primarily I feel I need to conclude by noting these doubts. Leading with kindness is hard; it's one thing to set out a vision for a kind culture but another thing altogether to enact and sustain it and to do the work repeatedly in the face of challenges to consistency, expectations, culture, and engagement. Brookfield (1995) reminds us that the sincerity of our intentions does not guarantee the purity of our practice, and this is a guiding insight for me in recognising that it's not always enough to want to be kind; instead, we have to create systems, processes and expectations that create the conditions for kindness. Our Collarts Way of Teaching framework provided us with a timely and relevant reminder of how we might put this into practice: by highlighting heart, authenticity and insight as framing principles for what, how, and why we work together. But it has also been instructive (and challenging) to highlight, reinforce and extend this framework through a period of increased uncertainty.

As a leader, this work is founded in trust. It requires an ongoing emphasis on process, improvement and refinement, instead of a focus on outcomes.

It means more than only ever enacting what we think is kind practice, to considering the ways our kindness is experienced by others. And perhaps just as importantly, it means understanding and empathising when kindness is absent. In my (admittedly relatively brief) time leading an educational institution, it's never been harder than it is right now to lead for kindness. At the same time, it's never been more important to do so.

References

Brookfield, S. (1995). *Becoming a critically reflective teacher*. Hoboken, NY: John Wiley & Sons.

Denial, C. (2019, August 15). A pedagogy of kindness. *Hybrid Pedagogy*. https://hybridpedagogy.org/pedagogy-of-kindness/

Hews, R., McNamara, J., & Nay, Z. (2022). Prioritising lifeload over learning load: Understanding post-pandemic student engagement. *Journal of University Teaching & Learning Practice, 19*(2), 128–146. https://doi.org/10.53761/1.19.2.9

Chapter 10

Sustaining others without starving yourself

Educator wellbeing, compassion, kindness and self-care

Alan Borthwick OBE, Mark Cole, Sandra Grace, Jeff Janowick and Samantha Chang

Introduction

Teaching can mean taking students on transformational and often confronting learning journeys and is thus a demanding profession. The challenges can drain educators' goodwill and vitality. As one colleague said, 'I don't have time to connect, let alone be kind. All I do is shuffle students through content and hope for the best.' In these times it is vital that the educator has a solid self-knowledge and system of care to help them maintain their wellbeing and resilience.

This chapter contains five case studies in which educators share stories of how they maintain their composure, resilience, passion and empathy for teaching and their students in light of institutional pressures, negative student evaluations and a host of other challenges. In each case study, the author/s share strategies that assisted them to maintain kindness and an ethic of care for themselves and their students in their daily work.

Kindness and respect cost nothing but mean everything

Alan Borthwick OBE and Mark Cole

Introduction

As two former colleagues who worked in the Faculty of Health Sciences at the University of Southampton (one of the UK's Russell Group institutions), we shared many experiences teaching undergraduate and postgraduate students, whilst also grappling with the multi-layered institutional prioritisation of staff research performance, course/programme management and effective teaching. Whilst both of us are now retired, one continues to hold an Emeritus Professor position, involving periodic occasional teaching to undergraduate students and some research activity, and the other still advises on programme leadership and

DOI: 10.4324/9781003364887-10

management. In combination, we have many years of experience in higher education, research, management, and clinical work. Although both of us were originally allied health clinicians, by the end of our careers, we had attained the positions of Professor and Principal Teaching Fellow respectively. The former focused on both research and teaching, the latter on teaching, course leadership and staff team management. Both had attained qualifications in teaching practice, as well as a range of higher academic degrees and professional fellowships. Each of us presents a case study highlighting the importance of kindness and self-care.

Throughout the entire period of our employment at the University, the key challenges remained the same: balancing institutional expectations of research activity and performance with high-quality teaching and learning at both the undergraduate and postgraduate levels. Research active staff were, naturally, focused on prioritising research grant applications, funded research studies and publishing academic journal papers. Teaching was perhaps regarded by some as an unwelcome distraction and research-focused staff on occasion sought to minimise teaching commitments in order to devote time to securing research grant awards. However, there was a notable shift in organisational ethos over the last decade of our service, with the introduction of a new staff promotion academic structure designed to acknowledge an academic equivalence between teaching and research.

At the same time, there were added pressures placed on academic staff in terms of student support. Student surveys had increasingly exposed a decline in support, with a drop in student satisfaction. Economic considerations also played a part, leading to several rounds of voluntary severance offers, placing greater pressure on those who remained. Student recruitment also became increasingly competitive, both nationally and internationally, impacting student numbers.

Our values and approaches to student learning and staff wellbeing have been, in no small measure, shaped by one of our senior professional colleagues, whose philosophy of practice emphasises the importance of kindness, captured in one of his maxims, that "leadership at every level should inspire, encourage, challenge and support. Kindness and respect cost nothing but mean everything." To him we owe a debt of gratitude,[1] as we do to our long-standing Head of Department, whose compassion, wisdom and advice were invaluable.[2]

In our case exemplars, we draw on our own personal experiences and initiatives rather than any embedded institutional policies. Of course, there remain key institutional initiatives to safeguard the wellbeing of students and staff, but organisations need the empathy and understanding of individuals to interpret the rules with thoughtfulness and care. Surviving the harsh world of academia so often depends on the benevolence and foresight of good leaders and effective managers and we feel our case exemplars illustrate this point.

Case study 1

On occasion, staff may be vulnerable to accusations of failing to do enough to support students. On one occasion I was asked to meet with a student along with the Head of Department, to discuss progress, given the student had not been performing as well in recent months and the exam period was quickly approaching. It was a Friday, just before the weekend. He seemed a little hesitant, quiet and even slightly distracted. Although a very amiable and good student as a rule, we were aware his academic performance had dipped recently. As he needed to travel back to his parents' house that afternoon, he was clearly in a hurry to depart to catch the London-bound coach. So, we arranged to meet him again the following week and, after a brief conversation, let him go so that he would not be late. On the following Monday, we learned that his parents had lodged a complaint that we had allowed their son to leave the university and travel to London on his own, given that on the journey home he had experienced a psychotic episode that had necessitated his admission to hospital over the weekend. The parents felt that we should have detained their son for his own safety. However, neither of us was a qualified psychiatrist and certainly had no authority to detain him, nor could we be reasonably expected to anticipate an impending psychotic episode, as for us, there had been no clear indication of any such prospect at the time he departed. As a result, we were both required to attend a formal investigation before a senior member of the faculty and be questioned on our actions, judgement and motivations. It was, in truth, a difficult experience – but clearly necessary to establish what had happened and what lessons might be learned from it all. Fortunately, the student received treatment successfully and was able to return to his studies. The Head of Department and I were subsequently asked to act as his final clinical examiners (it had been delayed whilst he responded to treatment). We agreed, and the student passed. He subsequently used us both as referees for job applications following graduation and did so again in later years when applying to study for a master's degree at another university. Although bruised by the experience of a complaint and an investigation, we supported each other and took time to chat it over and re-examine our actions. We acted as a mirror for each other and tried to view the episode as a learning experience. For me, the wisdom, calm and empathy of the Head of Department enabled me to accept the events as part of the responsibility of being an academic, whilst also recognising its boundaries and limitations.

Case study 2

The life of an academic by definition is full of acute and longer-term challenges from a wide-ranging source reservoir. The overarching political and economic climate shapes the manner in which institutions form their own strategic direction. The quasi-independent educational philosophy of the national and international marketplace influences the global demand for highly skilled graduates to demonstrate validity in a progressive society. A university education is often seen as a panacea for career success and financial security. Obtaining a first-class degree now seems to be the goal for all students and as a result expectations from parents/guardians/sponsors and students have continued to rise. Often, many of these factors can have positive influences and associated outcomes, but academics tend to be held fully responsible for every aspect of educational policy and delivery. Therefore, at times, it can feel as though in the circus of public opinion, you are seen as the ringmaster and the clown.

One of the times of greatest challenge occurred after a round of voluntary severance to readjust the fiscal equilibrium of the institution. For those of us associated with leading and teaching healthcare programmes, this was against the backdrop of a radical change to the funding model for healthcare students. The funding reforms terminated NHS bursaries which historically provided tuition fees and cost of living support. This was replaced by the standard support system which consisted of loans for fees and maintenance. The reforms were highly contentious and the effect was to reduce the number of students applying for healthcare programmes.

At this stage, together with reduced staffing, came the stark realisation that if recruitment didn't substantially improve, our specific healthcare programme would be subject to closure.

I think it's fair to say that together with what appeared to be our 'last rites' as a healthcare programme, I felt fairly downbeat as I realised my name would be forever associated with the closure. Of course, the students on the programme had every right to expect a continuous high-quality experience preparing them for the rigours of clinical practice, regardless of the issues the remaining staff were facing. For those of us who had worked in some form of public service, including the NHS, the issue of crisis upon crisis is a common theme. I also felt the key to weathering the frequent storms was to continue to provide the best possible delivery of services within the constraints and never gripe to the clients/students. However, the personal cost of such an approach can be detrimental to one's physical and mental health.

This is where the importance of support from wise and experienced colleagues becomes essential. I realised right at the start of the crisis that I needed to meet and speak regularly with two of my professorial colleagues who were fully versed in the context and the nature of the unfolding calamity. They kindly agreed to discuss my ideas of a strategic response as well as providing further networking opportunities with very senior colleagues around the UK who had in-depth political and demographic knowledge of how this particular policy decision would play out over the next couple of years. With such support, my feeling of isolation was replaced by a resolve to see the crisis as an opportunity for change: to refocus our recruitment efforts and realign the programme objectives to fit the needs of international requirements and increasing specialism in the UK. Over the next two years, recruitment to the programme recovered, and the changes to the design and delivery of the curriculum were well received by students, sponsors and employers. It is very clear to me that without the support of my colleagues, the outcome of the crisis could have been very different.

As part of the governance process and to ensure the quality of the specific healthcare programme I was leading, student feedback regarding all aspects of the teaching and learning environment was actively encouraged. The process consisted of academic staff meeting formally with student representation from each year group together with other students representing special interests on a bimonthly basis. Over the years, this arrangement had worked very well, and it enabled the staff to respond to concerns quickly and effectively and make the necessary changes as required. However, during one particularly difficult period, an overly assertive student representative tended to raise issues in an extremely critical and aggressive way. The person also sought to disparage specific staff regarding their teaching style and marking abilities. This was often timed immediately after marks had been received following the end of a module. The person tended to garner support from those students who hadn't achieved particularly high scores. The effect of such persistent negativity certainly caused some initial distress within the staff group, and I felt this acutely. I recognised that the student probably had been thrust into this position and was trying to represent the student body but didn't have the necessary skills to achieve this in a professional manner, so the aggression spilled over into the dialogue.

In consultation with the staff team, I decided to meet with all the student representatives and provide more detail on the structure and processes of the programme together with the overarching governance requirements. I was also able to demonstrate how all aspects of the programme prepared students for real-life working environments, including dealing with challenges, limitations and disappointments. At subsequent student representative meetings, we provided much more explanation of specific constraints that were outside of our control. We shared improvement plans and took more time to allay concerns. Over time, we saw a significant change in the previously antagonistic manner of the student. By helping develop a wider and deeper understanding of the programme and its objectives, the student matured into a well-rounded professional and finally, we were very pleased to provide a positive reference for future employment. In this instance, staff working together to solve a difficult problem and refusing to be deflected, despite the feelings of injustice, showed the mark of true kindness and professional behaviour.

To do so takes effort and, often, courage. Both our case studies illustrate the need for, and the benefit of, kindness in the academic world.

Digging myself out of a hole: The importance of reflective practice for sustaining compassionate self-care

Sandra Grace

My story is about receiving negative student feedback, my reaction to it, and how I learned to be compassionate to myself and my students. Many universities use formal student feedback questionnaires at the end of each semester to evaluate teacher effectiveness and student satisfaction with various aspects of their courses (Heffernan & Bosetti 2021). Teachers experience a range of reactions to these comments, including elation, rationalisation, denial, and defensiveness (Moore & Kuol, 2005). Students have the opportunity to write anonymously which may account for the 'high prevalence of offensive comments' (Lakeman et al., 2021).

At this point in my career, I was relatively new to the university and was teaching a cohort of fifth-year (final-year) osteopathy students. This was the third time I had taught this subject, and I felt my delivery of it continued to improve. My brief for the subject was a big one – I was to give an overview of current evidence for mainstream medical diagnostic and treatment approaches to common health conditions, taking a different body system each week. The focus in this final year was clinical practice, and my subject was designed to support students' clinical reasoning. Perhaps because I had been trained in a different school of osteopathy, I was specifically instructed not to discuss osteopathic approaches, as that was taken care of in other parts of the course.

I'll never forget the day I received the report from the student feedback questionnaires, which included both a numerical score against the University average and students' comments. We were on holiday. I had taken my work laptop and checked emails most days just in case there was something urgent I needed to attend to (not a habit I recommend but something I am in the habit of doing). When the student feedback arrived for this particular subject, I opened it expecting to read the positive feedback I was used to. I was shocked and very hurt to read some of the comments. One student's comments were particularly hurtful. The student questioned my osteopathy qualifications and my fitness to teach the subject. I fought back tears and couldn't speak about it, not even to my travel partner (my closest confidante and the person who always provided a sympathetic ear and good advice when I needed it). It took a few days before I could talk about it without bursting into tears. I tried to guess who the student might have been and wondered how they could possibly have doubted my qualifications and expertise. To make matters worse, at the time I was spending about 20 hours a week preparing the 4-hour lecture and tutorial. (Over the years, I did get a little more efficient at preparing the subject, but the content always needed updating. The last time I taught the subject, I had it down to 6 or 7 hours per week to locate, critically appraise and incorporate the latest research findings into my teaching – I was pretty happy with that).

Eventually I reached a point at which I could talk about the negative feedback I had received with my confidante. I thought I knew who the anonymous student in question might be, remembering one time in class when the student was promoting the value of energetic healing and I commented that, in the absence of evidence, my position was to be open to but sceptical of such alternative healing approaches. I rationalised that perhaps this had really upset the student. I was also preparing a promotions application at the time and I remember thinking, 'There goes my promotion', with such a low teaching effectiveness score and negative comments. However, once I'd had time to get over the shock, I was able to enjoy the rest of my holiday (although I did continue to check my email each day).

As fortune had it, I had the same group of students for the following semester. I debated with myself about the wisdom of just getting on with the new semester or whether I should talk to the students about the feedback. I decided to talk to them. In my first class, I thanked students for their feedback on last semester's subject. I told them that I valued what they had to say and encouraged more students to respond at the end of the following semester, particularly because I'm always genuinely keen to improve the learning experience for students. I told the class that someone had questioned my qualifications and teaching and clinical experience as an osteopath. I wrote my qualifications on the whiteboard (I have nine postgraduate qualifications) and briefly summarised my teaching and practice experience. I also reminded them about the focus of the subject – mainstream medical, not osteopathy. All this only took up the first few minutes of the session and then I moved on with Week 1. On reflection, I don't know if it was necessary to provide this feedback. I also reflected on the students' comments about wanting a more osteopathic focus and took this feedback to the Course Coordinator. I was hoping to be able to integrate more osteopathic diagnostic and treatment approaches into the subject. However, I was encouraged to maintain the current medical focus, which I did. I'm also pleased to say that after that episode, my teaching effectiveness scores for the subject returned to normal.

In my promotions application, I acknowledged the low teaching effectiveness score from my most recent teaching. I talked about the importance of student feedback for quality improvement. I outlined the improvements that I planned to make. And I did get my promotion, despite the dip in teaching effectiveness scores that year. It highlighted for me the importance of reflecting on student feedback and making changes where appropriate and possible to do so.

It seems to me that there are lessons about kindness here. First, I had to learn to be kind to myself. I am a dedicated and hard-working teacher and have always endeavoured to create an inspiring learning environment. But I also know that no teacher can get it right for every student every time. It took me a while to come to terms with such negative feedback, but in time I did. I also kept in mind that scores from student feedback questionnaires and student comments may not be accurate representations of all students' views, although that's not what I had thought at the time.

Next, I had to be kind in my response to students. I tried to see the world from the students' points of view. There is always something to learn about ways to improve the student experience, especially from those you are trying to inspire, to expand their knowledge and understanding and their capacity to perform safely and competently in clinical practice. I learnt that responses to student feedback about teaching effectiveness, even to comments I perceived as unkind or unreasonable, should be compassionate, constructive and respectful.

Reflective practice is at the core of self-kindness. I know that when I take time to think about my teaching, things that go well and things that don't, I create an opportunity to learn about myself. Purposefully cultivating reflective practice has supported my ability to be resilient and to maintain my enthusiasm for teaching and empathy for students over a long teaching career.

Being kind to our students starts with being compassionate to ourselves

Jeff Janowick

If you are engaged in enacting the pedagogy of kindness, then you know it is a rewarding and enriching experience. You also know it requires a great deal of energy and resiliency. Just as we should be compassionate to our students, we also need to be compassionate to ourselves. This case study is a reflection on how I enact a pedagogy of kindness and how I apply the principles of care to myself as well as my students. My practice is shaped by my experience teaching general education History courses at a mid-sized community college in the Unites States with a diverse student population.

Acknowledging emotional labor

One place to start is by acknowledging that the pedagogy of kindness is a practice and that means it is work. Choosing to see the best in our students, to discover their strengths and to give them the encouragement to succeed requires emotional labor that is often tiring. Being intentional about trusting our students and treating them as people who are more than their role as students requires regularly reassessing our approaches. The pedagogy of kindness is more than just 'being nice'.

Building resiliency is also a practice. It is a habit we establish by intentionally applying the principles of our pedagogy to ourselves. Resiliency is not about having boundless capacity; it involves structuring your actions to be impactful without exhausting your reserves. We can include practices that encourage resiliency in our pedagogy.

It's important to remember that there is emotional labor to *not* using the pedagogy of kindness as well. *Not* trusting your students is exhausting in a different way.

The pedagogy of kindness as self-care

Practicing the pedagogy of kindness is itself a form of self-care. There is a reward that comes from treating people with care, focusing on their strengths and building a community within your classroom. It is a lot of work, but it is productive work. I often think of my practice of the pedagogy of kindness as saying yes to students. Some will argue that saying no is necessary to uphold rigor, maintain standards and prepare students for the 'real world', but saying no is a lot of work. It often leads to confrontation, disagreement and protracted discussions about why you are saying no and why their reasons for needing exceptions are not valid. That anger and frustration takes a toll on us and students.

When I get frustrated, I try to keep in mind that it is less personally costly than constantly fighting with students. It reduces stress, and that stress reduction is cumulative. Seeing students benefit and seeing their work improve, energizes me. Assignments that are turned in after an extension are often better than those submitted in a rush (or not turned in at all, leading to anxiety and frustration). In the long run, the energy expended on practicing the pedagogy of kindness is less than the energy spent *not* practicing it.

Know yourself

As you develop a personal pedagogy of kindness, be honest about knowing yourself. There are many ways to practice kindness; not all ways are suitable to all disciplines, courses, or instructors. The pedagogy of kindness is fundamentally an approach or a mindset. As an instructor, I make choices about what methods best suit my teaching. I add to those practices over time rather than trying to change everything at once, and in that way, my teaching evolves as I learn more about myself as a teacher – what works and what I can let go of.

Enacting a pedagogy of kindness means I am flexible with deadlines. This works great in a history class: getting an assignment a few days late (or even a couple of weeks late) doesn't interfere with the learning at the moment. It is certainly better for students to have completed assignments on time (chronology matters to historians!), but students can learn new material while they are practicing skills on earlier assignments. This might not be as true in math or chemistry.

Others focus on building community in their classrooms. I have colleagues who have built powerful connections with their students; at the end of the semester, there are high-fives and hugs. That's not really my approach.

There is community and connection in my class, but it has a different focus and reflects that I am more reserved. As my practice of the pedagogy of kindness evolves, I will add more intentional community building among students. But that is something I will develop over time, as energy permits.

Building community

Establishing connections and building community are at the heart of the pedagogy of kindness. This is true for instructors as well.

When I first shared my practice of this approach, I was pleasantly surprised by how many other faculty at my institution were already doing that work. None of us called it the pedagogy of kindness; we mostly thought of it as good teaching. All of us saw it as important to our teaching and to our mission (I teach at a community college, which has a focus on helping students succeed).

Those connections led me to reflect on my teaching and be more intentional in implementing these approaches. More importantly, sharing experiences across disciplines led to a campus-wide conversation about expanding our commitment to a culture of care in our teaching. With the support of leadership, we are also working to strengthen this appreciative mindset in regard to how we treat each other, not just our students, throughout our institution.

Being transparent

I find it useful to talk to students about what I am doing, and why. I don't think I have ever used the words *pedagogy of kindness* in class, but I routinely explain why I engage in particular practices. When I talk about extensions, I always explain that it is better to submit assignments on time, but I also say that I'd rather have their best work. If they need another day or two because they were sick or got called in to work or just didn't realize how much work the assignment was going to require, those are good reasons to request an extension. Recognizing that you need more time is a form of taking responsibility.

Explaining this helps students understand what is expected of them. This functions as self-care for me because it shapes their responses. Students certainly utilize the flexibility I offer; they also demonstrate a degree of responsibility in how they do so. The vast majority of my extension requests are for a day or two. Most students complete them within that time. That means I often get better work – which is both easier to grade and much more satisfying.

When students know what is expected, it's easier for them to meet those expectations. That makes my own practice easier. They also understand it is for their benefit, which makes them less likely to abuse it.

Be prepared for challenging students

Having talked about the rewards of this practice, it is important to keep in mind that there might still be students who lash out for a variety of reasons. It doesn't happen often, but it can be devastating when it does. I have received harsh emails from students calling me rigid and inflexible, suggesting that I could not possibly understand what students were going through today and that it was easy for me to keep teaching and grading and assigning work when the world was overwhelming them.

I was blindsided when this happened, because it was so at odds with my actual practice. To have a student be so angry was distressing. I was hurt but also feared that I had somehow failed them.

It takes an emotional reserve to not reply defensively or angrily when this happens, so be prepared to take some deep breaths before responding. Recognizing that students act in such ways because they feel overwhelmed can help us to respond with kindness. In some ways, these situations are the test of our practice. It is easy to be kind to people who are nice, to people who we think deserve it. We need to remember that all our students deserve it – even when they are not at their best. Often, they especially need it when they are not at their best.

It's okay to be tired

One last point: it's okay to be frustrated and to feel tired: all student-centered approaches require emotional energy. By the end of the semester, we can feel a little fed up with our students, institutions and colleagues. This isn't a sign of failure; it is an acknowledgment that we also need kindness and self-compassion.

Sometimes we think we're supposed to have bottomless capacity, but, of course, we don't. We all have limits. Knowing that this is true is important to keep in mind. I now recognize when I am at my limit and make adjustments in my teaching to reflect that. I'm less flexible at the end of the semester, and I tell my students that will be the case. I've had semesters when too many students were completing work late, so I enforced stricter deadlines. I told my students I was doing this, explained why, and gave them a clear date after which these assignments could not be completed. I don't do this every semester. It was an adjustment based on circumstances. Being flexible with myself and adjusting to my own capacity and the context of a particular class or situation has been part of evolving my pedagogy and caring for myself.

Conclusion

You've probably noticed that none of these are magic solutions. Most of them are small steps that have incremental impacts. Teaching is hard work. Building tools into my practice is the best way to ensure my own resiliency. I am drawn to a pedagogy of kindness because I want to take care of my students, but I cannot effectively care for them if I neglect myself. Building structures into my teaching, creating community and coming to know myself through reflecting on my practice helps me maintain my reserves and this has been highly effective in ensuring I also take care of myself.

Integrating office/student hours as a pedagogy of kindness approach

Samantha Chang

The term *office hours* is confusing. Are office hours the time when instructors are in their office doing office work? Why do syllabi list office hours? What do office hours have to do with me, the student? These were the questions I asked in my undergraduate years, and a decade later, I realized undergraduate students today still ask the same questions.

I teach the first-year undergraduate art history survey course at an R1 university in Canada. The first-year survey is a mandatory course for art history specialist, major and minor students, and a popular course for non-art history students fulfilling the university's breadth requirement. As a result, the first-year art history course consists of students across all disciplines and years – some are fresh from high school, while others are on the cusp of university graduation. Whether students were in their first year or their fourth, the confusion about the purpose and intention of office hours remained consistent. As the title of Margaret Smith et al.'s 2017 article highlights, "Office hours are kind of weird."

Office hours are part of the hidden curriculum and can impede student belonging and becoming within and beyond the classroom (Jack, 2019). During my undergraduate years, I worried about bothering instructors when they were busy in their offices and only attended office hours in my final year of study. The lack of interactions with instructors became a barrier when I needed to identify reference letter writers for grad school applications. While institutional guidelines state that information on office hours (*when* and *where*) must be included in the syllabus, the *what* and the *why* of office hours are often not disclosed in the syllabus or discussed in class. Now, as the instructor, I can reconceptualize and redesign office hours to promote belonging, inclusion and kindness.

Rebranding and integrating office/student hours

For the past five iterations of my first-year undergraduate art history survey course, I rebranded office hours as "student hours" and integrated these outside-the-classroom opportunities into the course marking scheme to humanize the learning experience and practice the pedagogy of kindness.

Rebranding terms, such as *office hours*, can confuse students who engage with the term in other courses. Instead of removing the word *office* entirely, I included both terms in the syllabus and invited students to in-class discussions on their perceptions, the institution's intention and my purpose for integrating office/student hours.

Office/student hours are a required component of my course. Each student will book and attend at least one ten-minute meeting session with me (worth 5%, first meeting only). In these short meetings, the student and I get to know one another, chat about course aspirations and worries shared in the pre-course survey, and connect as human beings. I offer sample meeting conversation topics in the syllabus as an FAQ, for example:

FAQ: What do we talk about during office/student hours?

Don't know what to talk about during office/student hours? The following are some ideas to get you started. Office/student hours are an opportunity for me to know you as an individual and provide one-on-one academic support:

- Your (and my) research interests and/or academic journey
- Class discussion/readings clarification and elaboration
- Assessment clarification and preparation
- Skills development and resource recommendations
- Academic and professional development strategies and opportunities

In addition, recommendations for books, music and videos (including TV series and movies) are welcome!

Office/student hours have long been recognized as one of the most underused resources (Fusani, 1994; Nadler & Nadler, 2000; Li & Pitts, 2009; Griffin et al., 2014). Even more concerning is that underrepresented students have even less access to and use office hours (Hurd et al., 2018; Byrd et al., 2019; Fowler, 2021). By integrating office/student hours into the course marking scheme, I am preemptively extending the invitation and setting the expectation that I will connect and learn about all learners as individuals. My focus is on human connection, which is the core of a pedagogy of kindness (Rawle, 2021).

Integrated office/student hours' impact on students

Office hours often seem disconnected from the overall course experience. Lake Ritter et al.'s (2021) study identifies five main factors affecting office hours attendance:

- Quality of feedback provided during the meeting
- Approachability of the instructor
- Scheduling convenience

- Proximity to a course event (such as an assessment)
- Availability to book extra hours

The integrated office/student hours approach incentivizes students to interact with the instructor (5% for the first 10-minute meeting) and attempts to minimize the association of office hours with a course event.

In 2019, before I experimented with the integrated office/student hours approach, 20% of students from my first-year course attended office hours. Since adopting the integrated office/student hours approach, attendance has increased dramatically and remains consistently high – 100% (Summer 2020), 90% (Summer 2021), 90% (Summer 2022), 94% (Summer 2023) and 95% (Fall 2023).

During the office/student hours meeting, some students come with prepared responses to my list of sample meeting conversation topics from the syllabus (provided earlier). Some students shared their curiosity about speaking one-on-one with the instructor, whom they usually observe from afar. Some students revealed their confusion about such meetings because there was nothing comparable in high school, while some wished they had engaged with office/student hours in other courses over their past 4 years at the university. Other students popped into the in-person or online space and stated, "I am here for my 5%." In each scenario, I invite the student to take some time to introduce themselves and help me get to know them as a person. Similarly, I introduce myself to the student and share who I am beyond the first-year art history course context. The office/student hours meeting offers a space for relationship building, intellectual conversations and human connections – elements for a pedagogy-of-kindness approach.

Student emails and course evaluation feedback reveal the value of the integrated office/student hours approach. In the most recent course evaluation data from the Summer 2023 semester, students wrote, "The mandatory office/student hour meetings really help to let me feel that an office/student hour is a place where thoughtful instruction and exchange of ideas happen." Another student shared, "Her 'mandatory' office/student hours were such a great time to chat with her not only about the course but any extra support I needed because of what was happening in my personal life." In my teaching practice, I want to support students holistically, and to do so, both the student and I need to trust each other. I often think back to Cate Denial's (2019) distilling of the pedagogy of kindness into two things: "believing people, and believing *in* people." In my first-year undergraduate art history survey course, 10 minutes is all that is needed to begin the process of believing and believing in one another.

Integrated office/student hours' impact on me, the instructor

A 10-minute meeting sounds manageable, but 10 minutes can add up when there are nearly 300 students. The fall semester at my institution consists of 12 weeks, with a reading week pause between Weeks 7 and 8. Because I wanted to meet my students in the first half of the semester to identify needs and resources early, all office/student hours meetings were scheduled in the first seven weeks of class. Between September 12 and October 31, I met with 274 students in 393 bookable meeting slots (some students booked multiple meetings). The nearly 400 ten-minute meetings equals 65.5 hours, which works out to be about 9.36 hours per week that I spread across three days during the first seven weeks of the semester. The scalability and sustainability of the integrated office/student hours were elements I carefully considered before implementation.

As an instructor, I want to demonstrate care and compassion toward my students, but I can only achieve my goals if I am compassionate to myself. Had I been teaching multiple courses in the Fall 2023 semester, I would not have been able to implement the integrated office/student hours approach in all courses. I was fortunate to have a team of teaching assistants to facilitate tutorials and provide assignment feedback in the first seven weeks so that I could devote my time to meeting students. After the initial seven weeks, I limited the number of drop-in office/student hours sessions and encouraged students to join the sessions in small groups to connect with me and others in the course. The integrated office/student hours approach frontloads my time and allows me to enjoy the increased feelings of community and connection in the latter half of the course. Each time I implement the integrated office/student hours approach, I am mindful of my capacity, and I intentionally redistribute my work, such as lesson planning and content creation, before and after the integrated office/student hours meeting weeks. In addition, I am transparent with students about how many meetings I am hosting within a limited period and students have acknowledged my time investment in connecting with each student and personalizing their experience.

I prioritize integrating office/student hours in the first-year undergraduate art history survey course because, for many students, this course occurs during their first term at university. For many more students, the survey course is their introduction to the discipline. Through the integrated office/student hours approach, I foster belonging, promote inclusion and model and practice kindness to my students and myself.

Notes

1 Sir Steven West, Vice Chancellor of the University of West of England, and former President of Universities UK.
2 Mr Mike Potter, who served as Head of Department for many years before becoming Faculty Director of Learning and Teaching.

References

Byrd, W. C., Brunn-Bevel, R. J., & Ovink, S. M. (2019). *Intersectionality and higher education: Identity and inequality on college campuses.* Rutgers University Press.
Denial, C. (2019, August 15). A pedagogy of kindness. *Hybrid Pedagogy.* https://hybridpedagogy.org/pedagogy-of-kindness/

Fowler, K. R. (2021). Are office hours obsolete? *Journal of Nursing Education and Practice*, *11*(7), 40–42. https://doi.org/10.5430/jnep.v11n7p40

Fusani, D. S. (1994). "Extra-class" communication: Frequency, immediacy, self-disclosure, and satisfaction in student-faculty interaction outside the classroom. *Journal of Applied Communication Research*, *22*(3), 232–255. https://doi.org/10.1080/0090 9889409365400

Griffin, W., Cohen, S. D., Berndtson, R., Burson, K., Camper, M., Chen, Y., & Smith, M. A. (2014). Starting the conversation: An exploratory study of factors that influence student office hour use. *College Teaching*, *62*(3), 94–99. https://doi.org/10.1080/87567555.2014.896777

Heffernan, T., & Bosetti, L. (2021). Incivility: The new type of bullying in higher education. *International Journal of Leadership in Education*, *51*(5), 641–652. https://doi.org/10.1080/0305764X.2021.1897524

Hurd, N. M., Albright, J., Wittrup, A., Negrete, A., & Billingsley, J. (2018). Appraisal support from natural mentors, self-worth, and psychological distress: Examining the experiences of underrepresented students in transitioning through college. *Journal of Youth Adolescence*, *47*, 1100–1109. https://doi.org/10.1007/s10964-017-0798-x

Jack, A. A. (2019). *The privileged poor: How elite colleges are failing disadvantaged students*. Harvard University Press.

Lakeman, R., Coutts, R., Hutchinson, M., Lee, M., Massey, D., Nasrawi, D., & Fielden, J. (2021). Appearance, insults, allegations, blame and threats: An analysis of anonymous nonconstructive student evaluation of teaching in Australia. *Assessment & Evaluation in Higher Education*, *47*(8), 1245–1258. https://doi.org/10.108 0/02602938.2021.2012643

Li, L., & Pitts, J. P. (2009). Does it really matter? Using virtual office hours to enhance student-faculty interaction. *Journal of Information Systems Education*, *20*(2), 175–185.

Moore, S., & Kuol, N. (2005). Students evaluating teachers: Exploring the importance of faculty reaction to feedback on teaching. *Teaching in Higher Education*, *10*(1), 57–73. https://doi.org/10.1080/1356251052000305534

Nadler, M. K., & Nadler, L. B. (2000). Out of class communication between faculty and students: A faculty perspective. *Communication Studies*, *51*(2), 176–188. https://doi.org/10.1080/10510970009388517

Rawle, F. (2021). *A pedagogy of kindness: The cornerstone for student learning and wellness*. Times Higher Education. https://www.timeshighereducation.com/campus/pedagogy-kindness-cornerstone-student-learning-and-wellness

Ritter, L., Scherrer, C., Vandenbussche, J., & Whipple, J. (2021). A study of student perceptions of office hours. *Journal on Excellence in College Teaching*, *32*(4), 81–115.

Smith, M., Chen, Y., Berndtson, R., Burson, K. M., & Griffin, W. (2017). "Office hours are kind of weird": Reclaiming a resource to foster student-faculty interaction. *Insight: A Journal of Scholarly Teaching*, *12*, 14–29.

Chapter 11

Conclusion

Airdre Grant and Sharon Pittaway

The narratives of practice presented here help us reflect on our assumptions and question our beliefs about the challenges and opportunities of enacting a pedagogy of kindness. Narrative as a means of examining beliefs and attitudes and as an expression of reflective thought creates questions, opens possibilities, and generates dialogue. In concluding this book, we reflect on the meaning we made from engaging with these narratives. In doing so, we invite you to consider our responses as two voices in an ongoing conversation about a pedagogy of kindness and to add your own.

Brazilian philosopher and educator Paulo Freire (1998) asserted that educators must risk acts of love and that education should aim at establishing a world where it would be easier to love. He stated that 'it is impossible to teach without the courage to try a thousand times before giving in. In short, it is impossible to teach without a forged, invented, and well-thought-out capacity to love' (Freire, 1998, p. 3).

Freire talks about love, and it is this which sits at the heart of the philosophy underpinning a PoK. We know many committed educators whose love of teaching, students and their subjects drive their practice. Our experience in higher education taught us that pedagogy doesn't just happen in the classroom, and so we looked to include as many aspects of the educational endeavour as we could. We invited educators to share their stories about how they enact a PoK in their daily practice, maintain their love of teaching and keep the joy in their work. When people are enthused by kindness and informed by rigour in their practice, institutional culture shifts accordingly.

We acknowledge the strength and honesty of our colleagues and their heartfelt commitment to creating and sustaining a pedagogy seated in kindness, knowing it requires fortitude and a faithful heart, something that is always tested in the workplace and utterly necessary in all human relationships. Individuals strive to enact a PoK in spite of the many realities which can be obstructive. Large classes, the changing nature of marking teams, overcrowded tutorials, rigid deadlines and other factors all work to erode faith and energy. Yet there is a groundswell of commitment to kindness, and this emphasises the

DOI: 10.4324/9781003364887-11

importance of supportive collegial networks. It's important to know that a PoK is an understanding of our own humanity as well as that of our students.

Enacting a PoK within the institutional framework of higher education is a subversive practice undertaken by individuals committed to fostering a culture of compassion and care within educational spaces. The narratives in the preceding chapters illustrate the transformative power of such subversion – an attitude of kindness which resonates with others and can help reshape the educational landscape. They also illustrate that a PoK is an action underpinned by particular values, beliefs and attitudes. It's a philosophy based on compassion, care and trust and a belief that students bring knowledge, understanding and their own set of values and skills to the learning environment. A compassionate approach to teaching is not only possible but also beneficial for individuals on all sides of the teaching–learning relationship.

The case studies give insight into the many ways educators strive to enact a PoK. One thing of particular interest was that some contributors, who had not initially considered their pedagogical practice as being based on kindness, came to better understand their own teaching philosophy by examining it, reflecting on it and writing about it. These educators now have a lens through which to share their teaching practice and to be more deliberate in their pedagogical decision-making.

The process of collecting stories has therefore made clear to us the vital importance of continued storytelling, reflection and sharing practice within the educational community. Dedicating time and space for reflection fosters an environment where the values and attitudes that underpin teaching become more apparent and intentional. There is undeniable power in these moments of reflection and introspection. Listening to each other's honesty about joys and failures makes us stronger as practitioners, encourages faith in the value of self-awareness and deepens our professional commitment to nurturing an educational ethos grounded in kindness.

We hope that these narratives serve as guideposts, encouraging you and those with whom you work to continually reflect, share and enact kindness in your practice, whatever shape that comes in, ultimately fostering more compassion, connection and empathy in the learning environment.

We finish by returning to the questions we posed at the end of the Introduction, and we invite you to add your own.

Why not be kind?

What might be lost if we enact a PoK?

Importantly, what might be gained?

Reference

Freire, P. (1998). *Teachers as cultural workers: Letters to those who dare to teach*. Boulder, CO: Westview.

For Product Safety Concerns and Information please contact our EU
representative GPSR@taylorandfrancis.com Taylor & Francis Verlag GmbH,
Kaufingerstraße 24, 80331 München, Germany

Printed and bound by CPI Group (UK) Ltd, Croydon, CR0 4YY
08/06/2025
01897006-0013